PRAISE FoR DEA

"Like grownups, children have stress. However, they often have fewer resources for dealing with that stress. Many keep their upset feelings to themselves, stuffing their issues deep inside where they will fester for many decades to come. Feelings that are not resolved promptly can cause illness, academic problems, social problems, and even spiritual problems. They also cause great suffering. Libby Kiszner provides an important venue for the education and healing of childhood emotional distress. By reading this valuable book, children can gain an insight into their own inner world and also better understand the dilemmas of their peers. The book provides a recipe for healthy emotional functioning that can lead to a definite boost in the emotional intelligence (EQ) of any child who reads it. I highly recommend that parents keep a copy of this book around the house. It can open dialogue, provide reassurance and information, teach an emotional self-care strategy, and much more."

—SARAH CHANA RADCLIFFE, EDM, C.PSYCH., AUTHOR OF *RAISE YOUR KIDS WITHOUT RAISING YOUR VOICE*

"This book is a wonderful addition for any teenager girl struggling to accept herself and her teen life challenges. Libby shares numerous methods to help teen girls create a transformative shift in their life. Highly recommended."

—BARRY GREEN, PHD

"Libby's column plays an integral role in the magazine. It is a spot where our readers from around the globe seek help in areas of family, friendship, and personal dilemmas. Her responses are always thought provoking and have really helped many throughout the years. Libby has acquired a marvelous reputation by children and adults alike."

—LIBBY TESCHER, *MISHPACHA JUNIOR* EDITOR

"Growing up is not easy for anyone. Just when you think you've got life all figured out, along comes yet another challenge that throws you through a loop. It may have to do with a friend or a relative or even how you feel about yourself. Which is why this book is so very important. Libby understands the things that bother you and knows just what to say to help you figure out how to handle the most complicated situations. After reading this book, you will realize that you can handle your unique set of challenges in your own unique way."

—RABBI NACHMAN SELTZER, INTERNATIONAL SPEAKER, STORYTELLER, AND AUTHOR OF TWENTY-SEVEN BOOKS

"*Dear Libby* strikes me as a wonderful work, addressing various anxiety-provoking issues which affect virtually all latency and adolescent girls. It is very readable and useable–and helpful for children and their parents. It deals in a subtle, sophisticated, but understandable way with very important concerns: relationships, bullying, avoiding ruptures, self-esteem, empathy, self-reflection, and proactivity."

—PAUL C. HOLINGER, MD, MPH, TRAINING/ SUPERVISING ANALYST AT THE CHICAGO INSTITUTE FOR PSYCHOANALYSIS

"I have no doubt that Libby Kiszner's highly relatable book, *Dear Libby*, will convince teens that their tough issues regarding friendships do not reflect a problem within themselves (as many teenagers tend to believe) but rather are normal occurrences—part of life's ups and downs—that invite them to grow, respond thoughtfully, and, most of all, stay true to themselves. Kiszner's book offers immeasurable comfort by reminding teens that feeling hurt, lost, or confused with friendships is something we all deal with at times. Full of terrific wisdom and practical strategies, this book acts as a guidebook, a compass to help teens to not just deal with their problems at hand but also develop healthy patterns, boundaries, and perspectives around friendships that can last well beyond the teenage years. Highly recommended!"

—ERIN LEYBA, LCSW, PHD

"I read this very sensitive, intuitive, and intelligent book that deals with the very important subject of friendships with such great pleasure. While the book seems intended for our youth, the messages contained in these often poetic and always beautifully articulated letters are timeless and accurate for people of all ages.

"We live in socially challenging times. Friends are often measured in numbers and by very superficial definitions. It is important that every young person understands the important lessons articulated in this book."

—ZECHARYA GREENWALD, DEAN ME'OHR,
BAS YAAKOV TEACHERS SEMINARY

"Kiszner shares a novel approach of showing young people how to deal with their problems. Her emphasis on the inner self is quite enlightening. And the examples of how to react to problems by focusing on the inner self will be helpful in dealing with the challenges faced by our youth today."

—RABBI S. AISENSTARK, DEAN, BETH JACOB
TEACHERS COLLEGE OF MONTREAL

"Libby has a wonderful feel for the pre-teen and young teenage emotional roller-coaster life! Her advice and guidance are sensible and wise and written in an engaging, straightforward manner. *It should be required reading for all adolescents and younger teens* or perhaps the source material for a class in school. In our challenging times, it's not only a wonderful resource for teens but also for their parents—a teaching tool to guide them in how to engage, relate to, and respond to their struggles."

—RABBI SHIMON RUSSELL, L.C.S.W.

PRAISE FoR LiBBY KiSZNER FRoM THE READERS oF THE DEAR LiBBY COLuMN

"I wish you'd been around when I was younger."

—F. SAFRAN

"Dear Libby has become a household name."

—C. EHRENSTER

"Although I am a woman in my forties, I look forward to your column."

—S. JACOBS

"You've made a quantitative impact on young people."

—Y. PETERSEIL

"Dear Libby, I love your column in the magazine. I always read it first."

—ANONYMOUS

"Dear Libby, every time I read the magazine, I turn to Dear Libby. I know that your column is meant for children and teens, and I'm in my midthirties, but there is something about your responses that is very empowering, resonates with me, and feels like it's rooted in truth."

—ANONYMOUS

"Dear Libby, how do you always know what to answer? Many times I read the question and then cover the answer to try to figure it out myself. But your answers always have a fresh and original twist."

—S.K., BROOKLYN

"Dear Libby, your answers are always loving."

—MRS. FELDMAN

"Most popular column."

—JUDITH FROM THE *MISHPACHA* PRODUCTION DEPARTMENT

FAMILIUS

Copyright © 2018 by Libby Kiszner

Published by Familius LLC, www.familius.com

Familius books are available at special discounts for bulk purchases, whether for
sales promotions or for family or corporate use. For more information, contact
Familius Sales at 559-876-2170 or email orders@familius.com.

Library of Congress Cataloging-in-Publication Data
2018937148
Print ISBN 9781641700184
Ebook ISBN 9781641700832

Printed in the United States of America

Edited by Michele Robbins
Cover design by David Miles
Book design by inlinebooks and David Miles

10 9 8 7 6 5 4 3 2 1

First Edition

LIBBY KISZNER

Author of Dear Libby advice column,
Mishpacha Junior

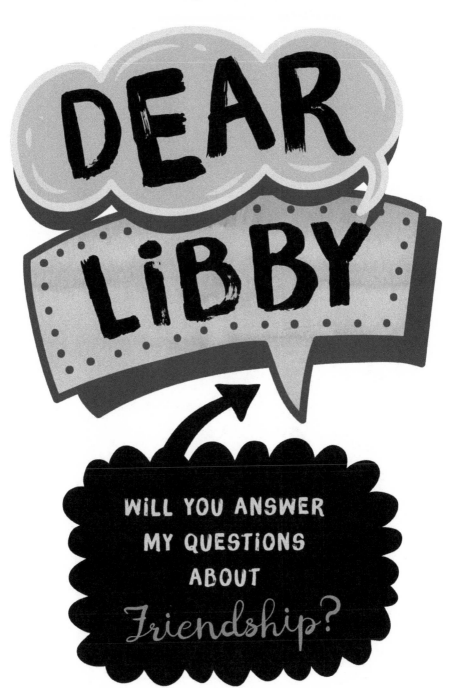

DEAR LIBBY

WILL YOU ANSWER
MY QUESTIONS
ABOUT
Friendship?

To my beloved children
Gitty, Shaya, Simcha, Esty, Yaakov, Yehoshua,
Devora, Moshe, Malky, Yossi, Motti
for the abundant joy you bring into my life

Contents

Acknowledgments

We don't accomplish anything in this world
alone . . . and whatever happens is the result
of the whole tapestry of one's life and all
the weavings of individual threads from
one to another that creates something.

—SANDRA DAY O'CONNOR

*T*his book is a product of the contributions of many people. I feel deeply grateful for the extraordinary support I received from family and friends.

To Mommy and Totty, Mr. Isaac and Leah Gancfried, two devoted parents, I give thanks for the gift of life and for your continued full and unequivocal support in everything I do. My father, a man of great courage, total commitment and uncompromising truthfulness taught me from a very young age to ask questions, to define them clearly, to struggle with them, to wait patiently for the answers to unravel, and to understand that the question is as significant as the answer. My mother, who is so encouraging and who turns her home into a garden of love and affection for me and my children, taught me by example how to live with authenticity and patience. May they be rewarded with every possible goodness.

To my precious siblings. You've added to my life in so many ways. Chavy, Moshe, Pery, Ari, Gitty, Shlomo and your wonderful spouses, your love and support mean more to me than you can ever know.

Baila Miro, for being my loving friend, cheerleader, and confidante, and my favorite person to laugh with. Thank you so much for holding my hand and nourishing my heart, for standing at my side with joyful, unwavering support through the entire process. My dear friend and colleague Tzirel Strassman, without whom there would be no book, no column, no questions or answers. You've added to my life in so many ways, and I will always be deeply grateful. Thank you for your invaluable help and suggestions through the various stages of the manuscript. Your gift of time is greatly appreciated.

This book could not have been written without many years of questions from my readers at *Mishpacha* magazine. Their courage to ask enriched my life and made this book happen. To all of you, my readers over the years, through whom I have learned more than from anyone else, my very deep thanks. Thank you to the amazing team at *Mishpacha* magazine and notably to the fabulous and talented Cindy Scarr.

Thanks also to my agent, Regina Ryan, whose wisdom and experience with publishers helped find the right home for this book. To my amazing editor, Michele Robbins, who not only is superbly talented at what she does but also is insightful, kind, and wise. Thank you. To Christopher Robbins and the fantastic Familius team, thank you. To David Miles for your excellent work on the cover, Kate Farrell for helping get this book in the hands of so many readers, and Leah Welker, for your joyful care in coordinating the details of the book; I'm deeply grateful.

My adored and delightful friends, among them Chany Twersky, Reisy Stern, Devora Lead Adler, Yocheved Rottenberg, Sarah Rivka Dahan, Dini Grussgott and Sarah Shapiro. Your friendship and support keep me going and make life so sweet.

I am blessed to have been guided by many amazing mentors and teachers in my life including Rabbi Wachsman, Rabbi Brezak, Hindy Kviat, Hope Stanger, Hanoch Teller, Shmuel Blitz, Mark Malatesta, Yonina Hall, Libi Feinberg, Mimi Zakon, Sara Chava Mizrachi, Bec Robbins and Leslie Rawlings, thank you for guiding me, inspiring me and generously sharing your knowledge and expertise.

I am especially grateful to Mr. Shlomo Bronner and Mrs. Ita Bronner, the embodiment of kindness. A very great thanks to you. You have transformed my life forever! In that sense, this book is yours. It could never have been written without you.

Even our thoughts are Divinely directed, and although we have the ability to organize our thoughts, to make our plans, it is only with the help of the One Alone that we can express them clearly and bring them to fruition. I'm deeply grateful and humbled to offer this collection of questions and answers with the hope that it will make profound, joyful relationships possible.

In Appreciation for 51Blue

This book has been enriched by the principles of 51BLUE and its founder, Gino Gross, whose scholarship, expertise, and guidance I could not have done without. I'm grateful to him for the many profound conversations and wise counsel that clarified the structure of this book and illuminated its underlying concepts.

51BLUE teaches an intuitive color-coded language of emotions and offers an innovative, down-to-earth, and scientifically grounded framework for understanding and regulating them. For more information about 51BLUE visit www.51blue.com.

Welcome!

~~~~~~

Dear Readers,

Friendships

*F*riendships create a shared experience, a "we" not just an "I." Two individuals can be as one and yet remain two. To love one another in friendship, means to see yourself through and in another person and to allow the same for the other.

The need for friendship and connection is essential to human fulfillment. When we love and are loved, when we spend quality time with true friends, we thrive and flourish. Friendships enrich our lives and remind us that we are not so many independent entities. We are each a living being in a world of many living beings, affected by each other, influenced by each other.

Our most rewarding friendships evolve through stages. Skill, practice, patience, and understanding develop richer and more meaningful friendship. Each stage teaches us something new about others, and about ourselves. Each stage offers its own rewards while simultaneously inviting us to step into a deeper, more trusting, and more connected friendship.

Questions

We learn about friendship, not from books, but by living it. Anyone who approaches this book with the idea that Libby has the answers and that she can show you how to fix your friendship issues in an overnight get-best-friends-quick-scheme will be disappointed. The purpose of inviting you in to the discussions about friendship is to help you explore the ideas and principles of friendship, notice the varying approaches to it, recognize the struggles and challenges that arise, and learn how to engage with those difficulties and not run from them.

There are different ways to read this book. You will meet different individuals, just like you, brave souls who were strong enough to reach out, to be vulnerable and share their struggles. Their questions can help you identify with the common strivings of every human being to seek comfort, guidance, and peacefulness. A personal question, like a story, carries a universal message. Its meaning allows you to see, feel, and experience another person's world. In it, you will find yourself.

This is the kind of book that you are likely to read and reread many times, because it asks questions that might surface at different times or different stages of your life. Reflecting on the discussions will give you the opportunity to increase your insights and understanding, so that you can apply the principles to situations that come up for you. Some of the ideas offer directions of thought that may take time to integrate and make part of who you are becoming. If you're not the kind of person who looks for immediate, quick-fix solutions, but you have the patience and endurance to gather long-term strategies, you can see these ideas as milestones to grow into.

This is not a book about answers. It is a book about questions. Questions are beautiful. They take you on a journey to explore different options, experience new things and adventures. There is no one answer, there is no such thing as *the* answer. Imagining that somewhere, somehow lies the answer to a problem is an illusion that we may hold onto in order to give ourselves a sense of security and certainty. Some answers are appropriate at some times and some for other times. Every situation is different and every person is different. The same person in a different situation or the same situation with a different person needs a different answer, so how can we give *the* answer?

As you read this book, check out the questions and explore your own answers—you are who you are. You know about your life and experiences better than anyone else. I invite you to wonder about the ideas I offer and see how they can add some wisdom to a question you are asking in *your* life. Sometimes people stop to tell me they enjoyed my answer in the column and ask, "How do you know everything?" I don't. Naturally, I hope that my words and ideas can be of help, but the responses to the questions are not THE answer, they are just AN answer. They are not the final word on any issue, they are just my understanding in a moment of time.

I invite you to see things differently, in your way, and to add your own understanding. Because, in the end, we are all on this journey of life together, walking through dusky valleys and sunlit peaks, and you learn to walk and climb through your experiences. The journey toward rich and satisfying friendships can be practiced only by you.

Sincerely,

Libby

SEE

Chapter 1:

See Yourself

My importance to the world is relatively small.
On the other hand, my importance to myself
is tremendous. I am all I have to work with, to
play with, to suffer and to enjoy. It is not the
eyes of others that I am wary of, but my own.

—NOËL COWARD

We all have a need to be seen, to feel acknowledged, to experience our existence. When someone's snide remark or mocking gesture makes us feel like we've turned into a pile of sand or vanished into thin air—as though our existence didn't matter, we can feel invisible and hurt. We'll do anything to avoid this pain: bending over backward and forward, going out of our way to please others, exerting time, effort and energy to ensure that we're seen.

It is this basic need to be visible and acknowledged that often drives us to do whatever's in our power to become extraordinary, outstanding, and spectacular, using all of our talents and abilities to be popular, to be a somebody—somebody who we think we're not.

Then, when we do manage to be in the spotlight, we soon discover that the moment is brief. It soon wears off. Too quickly we're out of "style" and someone else takes our place while we remain forgotten and unseen. Until finally, we realize the truth—most people don't see us for who we are, but for how they compare to us, what they can have from us or for what we have that they wish they, too, could have.

While it may seem lonely at first to accept that you aren't anyone's first order of business, it is also redeeming—your ticket to freedom. You at last discover that you have the possibility and the capabilities to see yourself, to experience your own existence. You become independent. No longer relying on the outside world to see you, to acknowledge you, to tell you that you matter, you learn to sense it from within. While the people around you will still do what they do, you will be able to consistently see yourself, and truly know that no other person can value you as much as you can.

You might know what I mean. You may have been called a redhead, a freckle-face, a class-queen, a carrot-top, a snob, a pretender, a wannabe, or whatever. You may have been flattered or teased or dismissed. But the only one who can really see and deeply know you is YOU. And when you do, when you truly SEE yourself, what other people say about you doesn't matter all that much. Suddenly, you realize that you're free. You, sensing your existence, is more than enough.

If you feel seen and noticed by yourself, you don't have to fear anyone's insulting comments. You don't have to stand on your head or do cartwheels on a tightrope for someone to see you. You simply know that you're here. Not with blazing, blinking, neon-colored announcements that squeal, "Look at me, I'm fabulous, I'm popular, I'm special!" but merely by sensing it.

Whenever you feel invisible to yourself and others, look around you. See the room you're in. Find yourself within the room and become aware that you exist. You actually take up space in the room. Take note of that. Feel the floor beneath your feet. Sense the air flowing in and out of your nose. Observe the up and down breathing movement of your chest and tummy. Give yourself a tight hug and sense the solidity of your own body. Experience your existence. Only then, turn to a close friend and feel how good it is when she adds to what you already know, "I see you, I know you, I love you."

When you see yourself and sense yourself, you can *be* yourself. That is your birthright as a human being. You don't require anyone else's blessings to be who you are. No outside friend or individual or authority can sense your physical existence the way you do or know the treasures buried within you the way you do or bring forth what's inside of you and offer it to the world, like you can.

~~~~~~

Better Than Me

Dear Libby,

I'm fourteen. I have a friend who is extremely talented in everything and in every way. She can act, sing beautifully, paint, draw, sketch amazingly, and even play piano. She's very popular and pretty and thin. She is so cool. I know that I'm not supposed to be jealous of anyone, but I can't help it. Every time I accomplish something big, she does it twenty times better than me. It's not fair that she has everything. Please help me fast.

Jealous

Dear Jealous,
If you see yourself for the person you are and you're not afraid that you will disappear into the crowd without being noticed as special, then you can be inspired by others. How do we become so visible to ourselves, that when others shine we feel inspired, not jealous?

We all have one thing in common. Something that makes us all powerful beyond words. You may, at first glance, think of it as cliché, but if you dwell on it each day for a month you will discover its wisdom. You, and every single one of us, has the most powerful device known to man. And that is your breath. First of all, we all breathe.

Your flow of breath is your flow of life.

We all breathe; therefore, we are.

The following exercise may sound incredibly dull to you, like counting sheep to put you to sleep. Nevertheless, if you're willing to experiment with it, you'll discover a priceless gift. Each calm and deep breath nourishes every cell of your body. It revitalizes your life. Breathing in is the first activity of your life, breathing out is the very last one. Everything that comes between those moments, the very essence of your life, is marked by the balance of inhalations and exhalations of air.

Follow your breath with interest and intention. Enjoy it, and you will discover its magical, unexpected effect. Very gently, it coaches and coaxes you into sensing yourself. It's the ticket back to yourself. When you can sense your own breath, you will never feel invisible.

As you breathe in, your awareness is drawn inward. Breathe out and you give expression to yourself. In and out. Merely by breathing with interest and intention, you will discover that you have a voice, a vision and talents of your own.

Once you can see and feel your own aliveness, you will be okay when other people shine. You can be free from the powerful addiction of comparing and despairing. Because each of us are different versions of the same living being pulsating with the breath of life. Clear some space in your mind to sense the vitality of your own gentle and rhythmic breathing, and you will be able to celebrate the lives of others. As your chest moves up and down, your muscles soften with each breath, and you sense the air flowing in and out of your nose, you will know that soon enough your essence, like a rose, will unfold and express its own unique vitality.

Sincerely,

Libby

You can manage one life—yours; nurture it with gentle breath, kindness and self-visibility to seed your own success.

Hated by Many

Dear Libby,

I'm hated by so many people, and I can't take it. My classmates act so mean to me. It looks like they think I don't have feelings, but really it hurts a lot. Please answer as soon as you can.

Feels Hated

Dear Feels Hated,

How other people act toward you wouldn't be so hurtful if you stop looking at them and start seeing yourself.

As you read these words, take a minute to draw your attention inward. Can you sense the flow of breathing moving in and out of your nose? Are you able to gently soften your muscles, drop your shoulders and relax your forehead? Because when you can do that, you can start exploring that wondrous world within you. This is who you are. Before anything else, you are a real, breathing, living being.

Once you find yourself and your inner world, you always know where to go back to when things get messy, harsh, or hurtful. It's kind of like knowing where your home is. As soon as you feel connected to who you are, and are happy with that, you become a true individual, the driver of your own car. It frees you to take charge of your own life and to grow into your best self.

I'm not saying it's easy to be in charge of leading your own life. We're not used to doing that. We've grown accustomed to sitting back and waiting for everyone else to embrace us in their love and acceptance. But that puts you in the back seat of the car. And believe me, it's a lot more fun in the driver's seat.

When you can see yourself and feel comfortable with that, the world sees you too. And likes you. If you meet yourself on the inside, others will meet you there too.

Most of the time people don't act mean because they hate you. For that, they would need to see the real you, and then decide that they don't like what they see. But they're not seeing you—the you who feels and cares, the you who hopes and dreams.

So, they don't know you. How can anyone hate you unless they see who you are and get to know you? And, anyone who can see the real you, doesn't hate you. Honestly, guys, who invented the word *hate*, anyway?

Clumsy seems more like it.

People are clumsy. They bang into you. They're brusque and rude and shove you in all kind of ways. It's not because they're trying to be mean, it's because they're partially blind; they don't see the real you. Wobbling and stumbling in their heavy armor, they are too intent on shielding themselves from other people who're not seeing *them*.

So be kind to yourself, is what I'm saying.

Please try to be kind to yourself. And see yourself.

It's not selfish to see yourself. When you know what goes on inside, you learn about seeing a human being—first you and then others. Indeed, the inner you, alive and breathing as part of every living thing, has difficulty distinguishing between you and your friend. It tends to believe that what you see in another is in fact what you see in yourself.

When you can see yourself and others, a calm joy exists all around you. That energy exudes a magnetic power that fascinates people. It's what draws them to you. They feel secure within it and they want to be included. When you feel comfortable with yourself, others feel comfortable with you.

Sincerely,

Libby

Seeing yourself allows you to feel connected to yourself and to others around you.

~~~~~~

How Can My Talents Become Visible?

Dear Libby,

I'm very talented and creative. I would like to use it in some way. The problem is that I don't have any true friends, just some by-the-way friends who don't really care about me. They don't know about my talents and won't pick me for the type of job that needs creativity (school captain, vice-captain, class president, etc.). Can you please help me find a way to get some true friends to help me bring out my talents and use them in the right way?

Talented, without Friends, almost 16

Dear Talented, without Friends,

You are raising a very important question, one that not only teens ask, but adults too. What do we do about not being seen by others? Everybody asks that question at some point in their lives.

We want other people to see us and our talents. We don't want to remain the best-kept secret in town; we like to use our strengths and give expression to the wealth of gifts with which we were blessed.

You're exploring how to get some true friends to help you bring out your talents, so that you get to use them. But nobody can know about your talents as much as you. So, the discovery of that search lies within *you*.

Like every human being, you carry innate talents that are uniquely yours. You have the ability to make a real difference in the world, whether someone picks you for a job or not. Recognizing your strengths and finding ways to use them is a responsible, challenging, and noble thing to do. But it doesn't require others to recognize you or your talents, and it doesn't call for impressive titles or positions.

It's you who needs to become the expert at finding and bringing out your talents. What's the point of other people knowing about your talents if you don't know them? Other people recognizing your talents is not the end goal. Self-visibility is important. Before you can put your talents to use, *you* need to know them. Look inside yourself and identify what you naturally do best. Practice, develop, and refine those natural skills. When you use your creativity and talents, to express that which is alive in you, you will gradually carve out a role that draws on these strengths.

Pay attention to the activities that give you a feeling of being in "flow" or "in the zone," where you feel good, you feel alive, you are in the moment. Become the observer of your life as well as the participant. Consider whether you become absorbed in a particular activity to such an extent that you lose track of time. Identify the hobbies that bring you satisfaction. Here are some questions you can ask yourself:

- What qualities or talents was I born with?
- What can I do so well I can almost do it in my sleep?

- What do I find fascinating, inspiring, and uplifting?
- What can I read about or talk about nonstop?
- What skills do I have the potential to enhance and master?

"Well," you may say, "seeing myself? That's not enough. I want to be seen by others as well." That's totally understandable. You want to experience connection and connectivity. Interestingly enough, there's something about becoming visible to yourself that seems to bolster friendships. The more you see yourself, the more others see you too.

People who have developed the ability to see themselves seem to acquire a magnetic influence that invites others to see them. Their own self-visibility makes them more visible to others. They don't sit and wait for others to come and unfold the talents they have. In the very act of experiencing their own capacities, they carry with them a glow and a vitality, a *joie de vivre*, which others find intriguing, making them curious to find out what else they've got to offer.

Sincerely,

Libby

 It's not how others see you that's important, it's how you see yourself.

The Royal Queen

Dear Libby,

I don't know what to do. Since I started school in kindergarten, until the end of last year, I was known as Class Queen. Everyone looked at me as a leader with an outgoing, fun attitude. I enjoyed the attention immensely. However, this year, a new girl joined our class, threatening my position. Everyone liked her, and slowly I was being pushed down into the dumps. I didn't like it one bit. Now it's as if we're both fighting for the position and I don't think it's fair.

Sincerely,

Wants to Be Class Queen Again

Dear Wants to Be Class Queen Again,

Your question is interesting, because you're asking to be a queen, when you ARE a queen, just like everyone else in your class is a queen. There is inside of you a queen with a depth of character guiding you toward your purpose in life. A queen knows that her main duty is to be queen over herself and to lead herself with elegance and poise, to respond with dignity to any situation, even in the face of a threat to her position. In fact, she sees challenges as opportunities for growth, to discover how to move with grace and nobility, whatever the circumstance.

A queen doesn't openly call attention to herself, and she doesn't go out of her way to get people to notice her. Even so, her poise and confidence draw others to her. When others speak, she listens kindly. And when she speaks, she chooses her words with care. She knows her self-worth. She knows she's a queen. She doesn't see herself above others or less than others but knows she matters and she always seeks to fully develop her potential.

A queen cares about her people—she wants the best for everyone. She is kind. She treats everyone with sensitivity and consideration. She is someone others can depend on.

There is no need to fight for the position of queen, because you already are one.

Sincerely,

Libby

 The honor and beauty of a princess is within. (Psalm 45:13)

~~~~~~

Be Who You Are, Together

Dear Libby,

I have no friends at all. I've tried so hard again and again but everyone already has their own friends and they either ignore me or act nice out of kindness. I can tell when they're not interested in me since they answer with short, to the point answers, and also, it's always me starting the conversation. Plus, I see them out of school with their group of friends, and if they would want to be my friend, they'd invite me, too, right? I have a visible disability, and I feel that's why no one's befriending me. But I'm sinking lower and lower into despair, and I can't take this

*anymore. I'm always alone. I don't want to talk
to my mum or anyone about this, I'm not sure
why, but I don't feel comfortable doing that.
Whoever I tell will always think of me as a
poor girl who doesn't have friends. What now?*

Friendless, age 13

Dear Friendless,

Friendship means that we can be who we are in a relationship. This takes seeing who you are beneath your skin, what you wear, how you smile, or what traits you display in order to belong.

A disability or a difference in visual appearance, can make it extra hard for others to look deeper. People are not accustomed to seeing beyond that which is simply in front of them, often staying with a shallow perception of themselves and of others. Someone with a disability or other life challenge often has eyes that are more open to what is usually overlooked by others. They see things differently than their peers—they get to walk around with the gift of real vision while others seem blindfolded. Contending with difficulties allows you to encounter the real face of humanity and see deeper than what the surface view provides.

It's easy for others to avoid looking at someone with a disability when they feel uncomfortable with it. But when it's you who's experiencing the disability, you don't have that luxury, and you can't help but see the frailties and limitations of every human being. Lacking the opportunity to run from that, you engage with it, you get to know it, and when you do, something happens. You come to see that which lies beyond the flaws and fallibilities of the human condition. You get to see the divine beauty and magnificence hidden inside every human being, regardless of their outer cloaks.

Despairing is often a result of comparing. Instead of looking at everyone else and what they have, redirect your focus and see what *you* have. Don't ignore your qualities and gifts, even if the whole world does. Don't wait for others to act nice to you out of kindness, get to it first. You, who have seen the vulnerabilities and suffering in life, will get to see the joy of empathy, compassion, and a purpose to care for others, especially for those who need help beyond their own abilities. You are not poor, you are rich beyond your imagination.

Sincerely,

Libby

 The biggest disability is the inability to see beyond outer appearances.

Never Sure of Myself

Dear Libby,

I'm always second-guessing myself. I'm never sure if I'm doing the right thing. When I go to school, I'm constantly thinking about if I look good, if my friends like what I wear. I'm very sensitive, and every comment goes straight to my heart, and I start crying. There are some kids in my class who couldn't care less about what others think. I wish I could be like that too. Please give me ideas.

Not Confident

Dear Not Confident,

It's natural to want to be admired and liked. Everyone has a different taste and some people will like what you wear and some won't. They may like certain things and not care so much about other things. That's how we all are. But if your sense of self is dependent on other people's whims, tastes, and moods, you'll find yourself on a very unstable platform. Like a seesaw, sometimes you'll feel up, and sometimes you'll feel down, depending on who you've crowned as the king who judges.

That being noted, there is a very significant individual, who has a taste, as fine and chic as anyone else's, who can see you anytime you like. The *you* who can observe that there's a part of you that's unsure if you look good has her own opinion, and that opinion counts a lot. This inner you is a valuable commodity. Hold on to it, don't be so eager to sell it in exchange for some fleeting approval. It's like an inherited heirloom that's always been with you. Someone comes along and wants to snatch it and run off. Be sensitive to yourself. Sensitive people, if they care, won't let anyone touch it. They know it's precious and rare, they can sense its importance. Be kind to yourself. Cherish your preciousness. Protect it in a glass container and choose what comments you allow entry, and which you will keep out. You are the keeper of the priceless heirloom.

Sincerely,

Libby

 You've tried waiting for others to see you and appreciate you looks, now try seeing yourself appreciatively and see what happens. ♡

I Think They're Talking about Me

Dear Libby,

I have a problem that every time I see other people talking, I think they're talking about me. I try to ignore it, but it doesn't go away. Can you please help me fast?

Insecure

Dear Insecure,

When you see other people who may be talking about you, you seem to forget that it's just as likely that they may talk about you even when you don't see. And so? What if they do? People talk. Today they talk about you, tomorrow they'll talk about me. That's just what people do, often to distract themselves from their own troubles. It's like eating chocolate to divert their attention for a little while from their own insecurities. Things that haunt them; things they're torn about; worries they carry and are trying to forget. Like chocoholics who always know where the chocolate is, almost sensing it melt in their mouths just by thinking about it, people fixate their attention on others.

Then again, this presumption may just be your own imagination. If it, as you write, doesn't want to go away, maybe you need to welcome it inside, give it some space and make it feel at home.

Better yet, harness its power.

It seems that fixations have power. The brain is certainly built to make any action, repeated enough times, into a fascination. If you bite into a piece of chocolate cheesecake and feel a rush of pleasure, and, if you're left with a lingering desire, you've started a trail of loving chocolate cheesecake in your mind. The more you eat, the more you'll want it. Guess what? You can use this power to start a new trail in your brain. Put your energy and focus into practicing something you want to improve. Write more; play an instrument; learn to tap dance. Imagine and think about it as much as you enjoy. Make it a part of your daily routine. Look forward to doing it. Instead of thinking and wondering over and over again about what other people may or may not be saying, redirect your focus to what you can say and how you can express yourself.

There's freedom in acknowledging your imperfections. It allows you to notice everything about you and to turn weaknesses into strengths by seeing them as learning opportunities. Accepting yourself the way you are, means you can see yourself, get to know who you are, and then simply express that in your own signature style. Perhaps all fixations carry the seeds of passion, the ability to devote yourself to something that will add joy to your life and the life of others. When you're focused on good things, you don't get sidetracked by what other people are doing.

At the end of the day, your life is in your hands, and it doesn't matter what anyone says or does.

Sincerely,

Libby

 Rather than indulging in negative thoughts about how others are expressing themselves, channel your energy to express yourself in a meaningful way.

Seeing through Your Own Eyes

 Dear Libby,

Until about a year ago I didn't pay too much attention to my looks. But since then that's all I've been thinking about. I look in the mirror more often and don't ignore anymore people's (innocent) comments. I started dreading going to public events. I'm not fat; I'm just really ugly. Now even in front of siblings and classmates I feel self-conscious about myself. I know I should discuss this with someone, but I don't think I trust anyone enough to confide in them. Please help immediately!

Ugly, age 13

Dear Beautiful,

Until about a year ago, you might have seen the world—and yourself—through the clarity of your own pure eyes. You were perfectly fine, created with your unique beauty. Then, it seems, you were impacted by others who, in various ways, gave you messages, that you weren't enough. What happened was that, like many girls who hit adolescence, you lost your own eyes and began to see through the eyes of others. You started to judge yourself through the eyes of society.

Clearly, this is causing you a lot of distress. You dread going to public events, but what you really want is to be seen, to be accepted, to be appreciated. The problem is that when we look through the lenses of people with narrow vision, it influences and distorts our perception.

So, how do you reclaim your own eyes—the pure vision you had before, and hold on to it? Better yet, how do you learn from what happened to make sure the way you perceive things remains yours?

Beauty is a perception. It's a personal opinion. Every person defines beauty in their own way. Every culture and era in history classified something else as beautiful. For example, in certain cultures, the words "you look so thin," was an insult. And historically, fair skin was considered beautiful, representing luxury and wealth, while tanned faces were distasteful, representative of poor peasants who worked outdoors.

The comments people make are filtered through the lens of whatever they're seeing at the moment. By whose standards do you want to define your beauty? By society or by the person you meet in the mirror every day—the one you'll spend the rest of your life with? This understanding can change your life. You can choose, right now, to see yourself, others, and the world through a broader, deeper view. You can make the decision not to lose your own vision when the narrow eyes of society's various influences are offered to you.

Seeing yourself from a wider angle means that you see not just segments of yourself but all of yourself. You are wonderfully you. All parts of you. Everything about you was created on purpose and with a purpose. Rediscover your beauty that's already there. All you need is for your eyes to see that prettiness.

True prettiness is an inner radiance that influences external appearances. A beautiful person is someone who can see herself, and be herself, comfortably, without working too hard to make a good impression. She is beautiful just the way she is. A flower doesn't bury its beauty beneath layers of makeup, desperate dieting, or other futile attempts to meet the narrow vision of others. It doesn't try hard to be beautiful. It just is what it is, in all its noble beauty.

Someone who sees herself and loves herself doesn't need to go on public display to be visible. She is visible to herself, because she sees herself, cares for herself and respects herself, and, by extension, others. This makes her attractive in a real way. There's a sparkle to her. She radiates warmth, charisma, self-confidence, and a deep sense of self that is so compelling.

Sincerely,

Libby

 The comments people make are filtered through the lens of whatever they're seeing at the moment. ♡

Pimples or Perspective?

Dear Libby,

I'm in eighth grade and I have a lot of pimples, and it's really embarrassing, and people tease me all the time. Please answer quickly, telling me what I should do.

Embarrassed

Dear Embarrassed,

Teasing someone who can see herself has very little impact, because she recognizes that teasing comes from another's narrow vision.

Teasing is a tool that some people use to make themselves feel visible and important. It's not about you at all. What significance do you give to what someone says about you when she doesn't even really see you? It just doesn't mean anything. If you don't respond to that person's need to be seen, to feel powerful and important, then the teasing doesn't serve their purpose, and it just stops. The purpose it *can* serve, is to remind you to view yourself with eyes wide open and see a more expansive image of yourself than just your pimples.

The more you see yourself for who you really are, the less the bullying will work on you. You simply will feel no need to respond.

Try teasing a person who is sitting peacefully and breathing calmly. You say something to irk her, and she simply looks at you with a kind and loving expression before, during, and after the teasing. Would you continue teasing her? Not very likely. Call it a starvation of teasing. There's nothing to tease, and so it ceases.

So why feed the teasers by seeing yourself through their eyes when you look into the mirror? These are very narrowed down eyes, zeroing in to one, very small, very specific feature of who you are. Have you ever had the experience of looking at somebody with lots of pimples who seemed unpleasant until she opened her mouth and spoke kindly to you? Chances are that when you looked at her again you didn't see her pimples, instead you saw a girl who was kind. When you spend quality time with someone and you get to know her a bit, she may seem completely different. Not because she has changed, but because your eyes, and your perception, have changed. Seeing through broader eyes offers a wider perspective; you see beyond pimples, to the smile on a face or the twinkle in the eye.

What a gift it is to be able to see beyond what meets the eye, deeper than external facades, wider than a pimple on a face. Such eyes care. They convey kindness, intelligence, and depth of personality. You can train yourself to broaden your eyes, and see a more elaborate, wider view. From this broader perspective, see yourself. See your kindness, your strength, and your beauty.

Then, when people tease you and make rude comments, you will regard them lovingly, with a gentle expression on your face. Your breath will be calm, and you'll remain unaffected by their words, but merely wonder what experiences they had that induces them to hurt others. You'll see yourself, not through the eyes of others, but through your own eyes.

Sincerely,

Libby

Practice looking at yourself and at the world with eyes that truly see, and you will develop vision that perceives far beyond teasing.

Embarrassed to Have a Social Worker

Dear Libby,

I have a social worker, and I'm SO embarrassed to have her. I know she's just trying to help, so I'd appreciate if you didn't just tell me that. Or that everyone is different and some people need social workers and some don't.

Embarrassed to Have a Social Worker

Dear Embarrassed,

Lots of people choose to see a social worker, a therapist, or a coach, because they want to enrich their lives. Maybe they want to be happier, gain courage, manage emotions, or learn certain life skills. They can reach out for support to practice healthy habits, develop themselves, or learn to use and express their talents. A trained professional can help you find contentment and self-confidence and explore skills to live more fully.

When negative beliefs and attitudes of others seep into us and get internalized, doing something a little different can make us feel as though we don't belong or aren't accepted. That's when working with a social worker can feel like a stigma. There's nothing embarrassing about getting the support you need. The real risk is losing your sense of self and your self-development out of fear that you might be rejected by others. Actually, losing your sense of self is a lot more harmful than losing the acceptance of others.

With this understanding you can use your discomfort to grow. It can become the catalyst that will help you discover more of your essence, mine the treasures inside you, and learn to hold on to who you are. Instead of focusing on others and what they think of you, focus on yourself—who you are and who you want to become. True greatness is found in the journey of constantly becoming just a little bit better.

The fact that you have a social worker means that you are brave enough to show up and get the support you need. Make use of the time you get to spend with your social worker to help you do that. Don't let other's opinions about it zap your strength from growing your own identity. If you discover and stay connected to your sense of self, you will then find those who look beyond stigma, or, they will find you.

As the popular quote goes, "Be who you are and say what you feel, because those who mind don't matter and those who matter don't mind."

Sincerely,

Libby

 A supportive person can gently encourage the natural unfolding of who you are and help you step into the greatest version of yourself.

Stop the Humiliation

Dear Libby,

I have curly orange hair, braces, freckles, and glasses. Girls in my class think that's nerdy, though I do not see why. I'm very sensitive and when girls tell me this I feel like crying. I try to tell them to stop humiliating me, but they just say, "Who do you think you are, Missis Freckle Face?" My parents spoke to my teacher who spoke to my class when I was not there. The kids then told me what happened and began calling me all kinds of names.

They Call Me Nerd

Dear They Call Me Nerd,

What a sweet and classical combination: beautiful red hair crowning your head, pretty freckles dotting your face, braces to make your teeth straight, and glasses to help you see! You are truly blessed to have all these gifts. If you can see yourself and cherish yourself, then what other people say to you will matter less. As you relax and focus on noticing all the positive aspects of yourself, you will have the inner strength to allow other people's words to slide off you.

Being called names is painful. It can hurt so much the pain feels physical. But no amount of name-calling can make you any less than the amazing person you are. In fact, every challenge met with courage helps you grow into a better and stronger person.

It's useful to be prepared for the next time someone speaks to you unkindly, by visualizing the encounter beforehand. When you're in a peaceful frame of mind, maybe before drifting off to sleep, or upon awakening in the morning, picture in your mind's eye, some girls calling you names. See yourself remaining calm and detached, allowing what they say to pass right by you. Imagine entering a helicopter and watching the scene from above. Observe everyone talking and gesturing and enjoy the view. When you stay calm and relaxed, exuding self-respect, you will gain respect from those around you. They will take their cues from your dignity, your positive feeling about your appearance, and they will treat you in kind.

Sincerely,

Libby

 When you treat yourself kindly you set the standards for others to treat you likewise.

~~~~~~

Left Out of a Friendship

Dear Libby,

I have a big problem in life, and I hope you can help me. I had a friend in school who I loved and she loved me. We were friends in seventh, eighth, and ninth grade. But in the middle of ninth grade, I became friends with another girl in my class. So we were three friends, and we had tons of fun. We had sleepovers and DMCs (Deep Meaningful Conversations). I just loved it. But now in tenth grade, the two of them got really close and left me out. I just hung around them and tried to be part of their conversation but then I kind of got the hint that they weren't really interested in me, so I went away and stopped speaking to them. Can you please help me? I feel so sad and horrible inside.

Sad

Dear Sad,

Losing a friend and feeling rejected is painful. Small wonder that you feel sad and horrible. Your friend was a part of your life, and now that she's no longer at your side, it can feel almost as painful as losing a limb.

Friends come and go in our lives. When a friend chooses to spend time with someone else for a while, that's not a statement about you and your worth. You matter the way you are, and you have infinite value. In fact, this in-between stage when one friend has moved on and a new friend hasn't yet arrived, is a wonderful time to make friends with a very important person: the one who looks back at you when you look into the mirror.

Get to know her. Have some DMCs with *her*. Find out what she likes, what she dislikes. What are her interests? What makes her happy? What are her strengths, her talents, her gifts? Hang out with her, become curious about her thoughts, her feelings, her experiences. Make the most of this private time with yourself now, because soon, when your new friend arrives, you'll be so busy getting to know her, you'll be glad you've given yourself the time and love you deserve.

Sincerely,

Libby

 Spending time alone with yourself can help you reboot your mind and refresh your life.

My Friend's Friend

Dear Libby,

I have a problem. My best friend became friends with a girl from another class. I was always friends with that other girl, but now that my BFF is friends with her, I'm scared to be friends with her or talk with her, because I don't want them to think I'm getting between them. How can I become closer with the other girl without making it seem like I'm stopping their friendship? I don't want to stop it, I just want to join.

Wants to Join

Dear Wants to Join,

Most of us read other people's minds—or believe we can. We see a look on someone's face, and we make a decision about its meaning: "She thinks I look weird." We hear a comment, and our minds quickly make up a story about that comment: "She hates me." Someone doesn't return a phone call and we instantly jump to conclusions: "She's angry at me."

These are all different ways our mind forms our own—often garbled—interpretations of neutral situations. But when we do that we are, in a way, crowning other people as kings and queens, and we submit all our power to them. Our life begins to revolve around them and what they think and how they feel. We begin to forget about ourselves and our thoughts and our feelings.

It doesn't have to be like this. Life isn't about the other person. It's about you. People will have opinions, and they will view us in many different ways, tell us all kinds of things, and behave in all sorts of manners, but their actions don't make or break us. It's the meaning we give to those behaviors, the stories we make up about them—how we think about them, how we feel about them—that determine whether they hurt us or not.

With this in mind, let's look at your struggle with your friendship. You have a best friend. Do you like her and appreciate her? Tell her. Do you enjoy spending time with her? Tell her: "I really enjoy spending time with you . . . I'd love to play with you or go out for a walk together or bake something with you. What would be a good time for you? Would you like to go out just the two of us or would you prefer if _____ (the other girl) joins?"

What happens if your friend says, "I'd rather spend time only with _____ (the other girl)?" You might feel hurt at first, perhaps rejected, maybe inadequate and not good enough. However, it is in our power to choose a different response—to stop negative thoughts in their tracks, by reminding ourselves to be skeptical about our assumptions, sense our own existence in the present moment and watch and observe. The only reality you see are two people having a conversation. What should stop you from joining them? The assumption that you're "getting between them" is a story you created. It's not a fact. At the same time, you might not enjoy their company. Then look around and see whose company you do enjoy. When you see and appreciate yourself, you'll know how to look for friends who see and appreciate your beauty and your qualities. Your friendships will then be mutual, satisfying, and enduring.

Sincerely,

Libby

 When a thought doesn't feel right, don't accept it as fact, question it. Ask yourself: Is this thought absolutely true?

They Call Me Names

Dear Libby,

My problem is my hair. It's bright orange and very frizzy. My friends sometimes call me names, like carrot top or tomato head. This makes me feel bad, and my face turns red, and then they say, "There goes the fire truck, her face is as red as her hair." My sisters also do this. Sometimes I feel like crying.

Orange

Dear Orange,

Every follicle of your bright orange hair is a special, beautiful gift you were born with. It's your noble crown. Be proud of it! Enjoy it.

You are valuable and precious regardless of the color of your hair. You are worthy even if your face turns red, others insult you, your hair is frizzy, or your hair has been cut too short! Do not accept as truth the taunting and teasing of your classmates and siblings.

In addition, you can always speak your mind and say, "It doesn't feel good to me when you talk about my hair in this way. Please stop."

Sincerely,

Libby

 To speak insulting words is in itself an insult—don't take those words to heart.

What You Can Do

Find the opportunity: Remember that you can have the freedom to choose your response. See the teasing as noise made by those who have nothing better to do. This is your chance to develop your ability to stay focused in the face of a lot of noise. Draw your attention to your breath and sense softness in your body as you watch their movements, while disregarding the content of what they're saying. Get very technical about it. Are they speaking fast or slow? How's the pitch and volume of their sound? Observe all this as though you would be a scientist exploring the way sound and movements work.

Discover the truth of who you are: Take time away from the teasing to remind yourself of the many gifts you've been blessed with and how lovable you are. Imagine that you're writing an ad for a babysitting job and list the ten top reasons why you would be a great person to have around. If you get stuck, just think about the nice things others say about you. Are you kind, friendly, considerate, funny? Write them down. Your list can fill a book, but for this exercise, choose ten that reflect the very best of you. Hang up this list near your bed, or on your mirror. Twice a day for the next two weeks, stand in front of the mirror with a big smile on your face and read the list. It might feel awkward in the beginning but see if you can have fun with it anyway.

Don't take it to heart: Consider that when you laugh the world laughs with you, when you love and appreciate yourself—that too is mirrored back to you. If you begin to take your classmates' comments less seriously, they may soon catch on and find something else to be busy with.

Final Thoughts

Your Intrinsic Value

Your sense of *intrinsic value* is based on what you think and feel about yourself, not what someone else thinks or feels about you. Take some time to contemplate the question: What is my intrinsic value, independent of how others see me?

Write your thoughts below.

For example:

What I value about myself is the compassion I feel for people.

What I value about myself is: _____

_____

_____

What I value about myself is: _____

_____

_____

What I value about myself is: _____

_____

_____

Inventory of Talent

Take out your art supplies. Drawing paper or markers, modeling clay, or paint. Without concerning yourself with the artistic merits of your designs, create a representation of some or all of the following: your talents, your skills, your dreams. There is not right or wrong way of doing this. Allow yourself to be playful and to have fun.

When you are finished, take out your journal and ask yourself:

1. What have I been reluctant to see or enjoy about myself?

_____

_____

_____

2. What do I want to enhance in some way? What are some qualities and strengths I'm already good at and would like to focus on?

_____

_____

_____

3. What are some activities I find fascinating, inspiring, and uplifting? What could I learn, read or talk about incessantly?

_____

_____

_____

~~~~~~

Make It Yours

Make your heart sing. Create a soundtrack for this next extraordinary chapter in your life by making a playlist of songs. Choose songs that remind you of your strength, your power, your courage, and your confidence—you can even write your own song!

CARE

Chapter 2:

Care for Yourself

**I am not afraid of storms, for I am
learning how to sail my ship.**

—LOUISA MAY ALCOTT

*I*t's nice when friendships coast along and you enjoy the fun and play and meaningful conversations, the love and laughter and even the tears. You feel the comfort of a tender heart that cares; you celebrate each other's existence and enjoy one another's company. Whatever you do, wherever you go, you know your friend is rooting for you, will stand by you, cheer you on when you're unsure, rejoice in your successes, and feel with you in your pain. You've created trust, petal by delicate petal, and you've come to know the softness and beauty of sharing your deepest thoughts and feelings. Life with a loyal friend at your side is a blessing.

Except, this picture-perfect depiction of friendship doesn't always fit with the reality right in front of you. A close friend who means the world to you, ignores you. Or, she doesn't agree with your ideas. Or, she makes a comment that stings. What happens then? Does your world fall apart? This miraculous, marvelous spark of friendship— wherever it comes from—does not always keep regular hours.

Your friend may be feeling down. She may have a headache. She may be so caught up in her own insecurities she doesn't have two seconds to worry about yours, and so she may inadvertently say or do things that feel rejecting or belittling to you when she didn't mean that at all.

When expectations in friendships are too high, and you hang on to your friend as though your life depends on her, there's a great burden on the friendship.

If you look to your friend as the air that you breathe, the stability of your life, the one and only caretaker, it is no longer a friendship, but more like a search for unconditional love, which is akin to asking to be adopted, held, and cared for. Your friend is clearly not the air that you breathe. You breathe for yourself. *Your life is entirely up to you.*

Sure, things happen in life that make us feel out of breath for a while, and that's okay, and we help each other out, but that's only for a time, not day in and day out. We need to feel loved and lovable regardless of what our friends are offering us, or how they feel about us at a given moment.

Every friendship has a natural ebb and flow, like the shifting tides of the sea. During high tides, our friendship boats sail along leisurely, buoyed by mutual vibrancy, and when the tides are low, it can bob and bump and crash and easily get caught in rocks and corals and reefs.

What keeps the tide high and our friendship boats safely afloat? The capacity to care for yourself, the unquestionable knowing that there is always someone at your side: *You.* It is you who can shake yourself free of the idea that your friend is the air that you breathe. You need to be your own best friend first. Because your friendship needs the freedom and the space to allow each other to be there and not be there, to connect and to disengage, to weave comfortably in and out of distance and closeness.

And unless you fill yourself up by caring for yourself, you will feel desperate. There will be an underlying current of intensity and urgency in the friendship that will create disappointments, discomfort, misunderstandings, and heartbreak.

On the other hand, when you care for yourself, not only is the friendship free to grow, but you also know how to care about another. Caring is an attitude, a mind-set, a way of being and acting, and it is within you. If you have the capacity to truly care for yourself, you naturally and by extension care for anyone you meet. You become a caring person. When you're feeling content because you know how to care for yourself, you're open to give and receive, to care and be cared for, to offer your gifts and enjoy the gifts others offer you. You're already fulfilled, so rather than being desperate, you're ready to listen and share and give friendship freely.

When your friend comes along and delights you further by a special surprise or compliment, you're pleased, but you don't need it for your oxygen.

In friendships and later on in life, in a marriage or in a working relationship, self-care gives a relationship the freedom to be primarily a mutual connection, a playful dance, and a beautiful space for freedom and expression and growth.

~~~~~~

Being Nice to Everyone

Dear Libby,

I try to be nice to everyone. It makes me feel great to help people. I want to be a good person, and I know it's the right thing to do. So, I am very nice to everyone, and I always try to help them. The problem is that some people just don't know when to stop. They call me all the time, and I have to spend such a long time on the phone with them to help them with their homework. They always need me to help them study, and they are constantly coming to me in school, so I can help them with schoolwork. They don't understand. I want to be a good friend and

help them. I want people to like me. Also, I
know that thank G-d, I've been blessed me
with the gift of being smart, so how can I
not help people?!?! I so badly want to be
a nice girl, so that is how I'm acting, but I
don't want to be a pushover, and sometimes
I get really annoyed. I try not to show it
because I want to be nice, but I can't take
it anymore! How can I be nice and not hurt
people's feelings without people constantly
annoying me and without being a pushover?
Thank you so much in advance! I hope you
can help me.

Frustrated

Dear Frustrated,

You are in a dilemma, because you need to be nice to everyone in order to survive, and if you're nice to everyone you can't live, because you get drained. Your energy tank becomes depleted, and you can't sustain it.

Most of us have at one time or another struggled with finding the balance of being kind to others and being kind to ourselves. In order to be a nice person, do I have to deny my own needs? If I ignore the needs of others, am I not a nice person?

Kindness is inclusive, not exclusive. This means that you as a person also get to be included in your kindness. You need to care for yourself as much as you care for others. For now, it seems the way you care for yourself is through caring for others. That's the long route. When you spend lots of time on the phone with someone, being nice or helping them with homework, their appreciation makes you feel good inside. It makes you feel cherished. What if you cherish yourself directly without having to use a go-between; an agent?

Ask yourself, "Am I taking care of myself, as well as everyone else?" If the answer is no, your energy tank is likely depleted.

Often it is easier to care for others than to care for ourselves. It can be challenging to say no to someone, even when that person steps all over you and you feel you need your own time. In this case, saying no, means caring for yourself. When you say "no" to somebody it means that all the care you have for others is now granted to yourself as well even if sometimes that means that you can't be there for somebody else.

Caring for yourself will enrich the way you care for others. It will be healthier, more measured and of enhanced quality. You won't be taking the long way around to care for yourself through caring for others; you will have the ability to say no sometimes, and you won't drown in the deluge of everybody's needs. Saying no to others to care for yourself will let you give more wholeheartedly to everyone, including you.

Sincerely,

Libby

 Only when you can care for yourself can you really care for someone else. ♡

A Good Deed Gone Bad?

Dear Libby,

I have a socially clueless (and therefore lonely) classmate. I tried to be nice to her as a kindness, and I'm afraid she took it as a clue that I'm her best friend. Now she won't stop tagging along with me wherever I go. It really irritates me. She keeps on interfering in my friendship with another very special and close friend. The girl I'm nice to is hostile toward my friends and is trying to break my friendship by singling me out and pulling me away from my friends. This is one big mess!! She copies my every move by insisting on buying the same sweater and shoes as me and begging me endlessly about where we're going to go "together." Please help me fast, it's urgent.

Upset

Dear Upset,

Sometimes it happens that we want to help people and they then start to express increasing neediness. In response to that, setting a boundary is an act of kindness. In this way we get to share kindness—a bit for her and a bit for you in a balanced way, because at times we cannot be kind to two people at the same time.

Being kind does not mean sacrificing yourself for someone, because eventually you end up hurting that person more. You have the right to set boundaries and to clearly let her know what is acceptable to you and what isn't. This way, you can continue to interact with this girl, but also have other friends that don't include her. True kindness entails integrity and honors truth. Your actions are in tune with how you feel; you say what you mean, and you mean what you say. Kindness without honesty is not really kindness and honesty without kindness is not really honesty.

A violation of boundaries is a violation of kindness, both to ourselves and to others. If we keep extending kindness to someone who willingly or unwillingly takes advantage of us, is disrespectful, or hurts us, the so-called kindness ends with conflict and resentment. It seems kind, but, in the end, you will drop her completely, and that will be far more hurtful. For kindness to endure over the long haul, you need to care for yourself, so that you can continue caring for others. Caring for yourself means saying something like, "If you want us to remain friends and continue spending some nice time together, this is acceptable to me and this is not acceptable to me."

Of course, it is then up to you to actually follow through on what you say. That means that when she crosses the line and acts inappropriately, you let her know. Setting limits creates the space in which kindness can happen. Truly kind people are those who are very clear about what they are willing to do and what they are not willing to do. They know how to say no and set limits.

It may be uncomfortable to say "No, I can't," or "I'm sorry, I'm not available," in the short term, but it's kinder in the long term. It will help you continue supporting this girl without giving up your personal space. Plus, she will soon come to see that you're not walking away, but that in this friendship, there is a balance of closeness and distance.

Sincerely,

Libby

Kindness is caring about yourself as much as you do for another, and you do so because you want to, not because you feel obligated or you fear the consequences of not doing it.

Perfectly Imperfect

Dear Libby,

My friends think I'm perfect, and maybe I'm a perfectionist. Everyone thinks it's great, but I'm really suffering. Whenever I do or say something that I feel is not so perfect, I go crazy. If whatever I do, wear, or say, is less than perfect, I get very frustrated and upset and guilty. If I get a mark lower than 100%, I feel terrible. When I say something to my friend that I feel wasn't so nice, I obsess over it for hours. Please give me advice on how to solve this problem.

Miss Perfect

Dear Miss Perfect,

Miss Perfect—that's a pretty large role to have to play. Truth is, imperfection is included in the very perfection of this world. Think about a handmade item—it's beautiful because of its unique imperfections.

Perfectionism comes from a belief that if we'd only be perfect, everything will be fine, we'll be loved and the world will feel safe. But this is only our imagination. In reality, this kind of perfectionism lacks harmony because it's an escape—a way of running away from the pain of being criticized or rejected. When we follow a dream, a devotion, or a passion on the other hand, we feel peace and a sense of flow. We become absorbed in what we feel passionate to create or express, like an artist who is deeply engaged in the masterpiece she is painting. She feels joy, not tension, as moment by moment, brush stroke by brush stroke, she hones and perfects her creations.

The kind of perfection that's an escape from pain or discomfort is when someone is in *survival* mode asking questions like, "How do I protect myself from the pain of rejection?" Another kind of seeking perfection is a pursuit of beauty and harmony. It's when someone is in the *living* mode and asks questions like, "How do I accept my imperfections while I strive for ever increasing perfection at the same time?" And, "How can I express myself in a way that leads to growth and development?"

In the living mode, you treat yourself—and that includes the critical part of you—kindly. Because you understand that the critic inside just wants to keep you safe. It stands on guard scanning the environment for danger. You don't fight the critic, you empathize and then gently guide yourself toward growth and expression.

Say for example, you say something you later regret, and you find that your mind is "attacking" you for making a mistake, don't "attack" it back. Instead be kind to it. Pause, take a deep breath, and practice soothing your mind with caring messages like, "I'm here. I'm safe. It's okay." you remind yourself that mistakes are opportunities to grow and improve. We all make mistakes (many of them!) and that's part of life, but perhaps the biggest mistake of all is to think that you are a mistake (which can make you feel upset for hours). You are just the way you are meant to be, on the journey of life, growing and evolving into the best human being you can become.

Sincerely,

Libby

 See your imperfections as learning opportunities. ♡

Three ways to pause negative self-talk:

The Bracelet Technique. Wear a bracelet around your wrist. Every time you catch your mind attacking you with negative self-talk, pull at the bracelet to remind yourself to meet your inner critic with kindness.

Gently Resist. When you notice a negative thought, don't fight it, simply resist it gently. Take a deep breath and say, "I'm here, I'm safe, it's okay."

Turn It into a Question. For example, the thought says, "I'm terrible, I wasn't nice," try, "What can I learn from this experience?"

When a Close Friend Sits Far

Dear Libby,

I'm in seventh grade, and this year I changed to a different school. I have one very close friend, and we sat near each other. But my teacher just switched my seat to the other side of the classroom. I don't know what to do! I feel we'll stop being friends since we're on different sides. I really don't want this friendship to end. Could you give me some advice on how to deal with this situation?

From a Newcomer

Dear Newcomer,

Friendships don't depend on how close or far you sit from each other. Two people can feel close at heart, secure in their friendship even when they're not with each other every minute. Friends are like bamboo trees in a grove: Even though they're standing apart, their roots are connected underground, so they grow tall and straight without leaning against each other. Though linked at their core, they have the strength and independence to be on their own.

It's ironic that when we feel too desperate for a friend, we risk losing her. When you don't feel that you can be there for yourself, and that you can be happy on your own, you begin to try fill that hole with friends. This sets up expectations. Expectations often lead to frustration and disappointment. Nobody can give you the care that you need as completely as *you* can. And you can. Because you can get to know yourself better than anyone out there. Care and nurturing is not only out there; it's something that you nurture from within.

For real closeness to grow, you first need to be close to yourself. Here are some ideas you can try:

- Imagine you're your best friend, what would you tell yourself right now? Look in the mirror and say it.
- Find little ways to provide love and attention for yourself. A warm bath? Moisturizer?
- Get to know yourself and what you need to thrive. Music? Healthy food? An energizing run?
- Take a few minutes to sit quietly, scan your body and describe what you're feeling.
- Write a daily entry in your journal where you can spill out your thoughts and feelings.
- In your journal, record nice things people say about you as a reminder when you need a boost.
- Think about what you're good at and find an opportunity to express it. Dancing? Helping others?

Your friend will feel a lot closer to you if she doesn't feel that you're desperate to have her, but that you're choosing to be her friend. Successful friendships are built by two independent people who come together and share themselves with each other.

The seat switch is a wonderful opportunity for you to connect with yourself. You can feel care for yourself even when your friend sits at the other side of the classroom. You are a whole person, even when you're on your own.

At recess, or after school, you can sit together and enjoy your connection on a whole new level.

Sincerely,

Libby

Give yourself the care you would want from others. For real connection to grow, you first need to connect with and care for yourself. 🤍

Nobody Cares about Me

Dear Libby,

Everyone just ignores me when I talk. My friends simply don't respond. Nobody cares about me. This really hurts my feelings. I can't say anything to anyone. Please give me a solution.

Ignored

Dear Ignored,

The need for someone to show that they hear you and care about you is normal. Talking is how we connect with other people, and yet, if you've ever seen two people trying to talk to each other at the same time, you'll know that while lots of people talk, few people listen. You're not alone, most people have nobody to talk to. Even if they talk about the weather and the price of shoes, the personal things stay inside, because good listeners are rare. So how can you meet the need for someone to hear you and care about you?

Fortunately, you already have free twenty-four-hour access to the world's most sophisticated care laboratory. Where is this lab? You're living in it. Your body is a state-of-the-art caring facility. In fact, it is highly caring and intelligent and has your best interests in mind. Your heart never misses a beat and your lungs are always breathing in and out. Even when others are ignoring you, or your friends don't respond to what you say, or your feelings get hurt, your heart's four little chambers go right on pumping and your lungs continue to expand and contract.

It's worth taking the time to explore your body's unique care system. Its instinctual wisdom and responsiveness will surprise you. Though we're accustomed to paying attention to everyone around us, it can be interesting to pay attention to what's going on beneath our own skin.

Before anything else, you are a physical existence. You are a person simply because you are located in your body, a body that is very present, here and now. If you take a look at your arms and sense them, you will notice something powerful about yourself. If you feel your feet touching the ground, you will sense that you have a strong base to your existence. If you gently stroke your face, you can experience yourself as a concrete, tangible being. You are uniquely you and no one else.

This body of yours is a very solid, tangible existence. And it breathes.

Drawing attention to your breath and softening muscles is an act of care. You are nourishing your mind and body, you are able to slow down and gain a sense of who you are.

Take a moment to relax into your body. Close your eyes. How do you feel? Your body is full of sensations ranging from warmth to coolness, tingling, tightness, pulsing—responses to various stimuli. Listen to it. Care about it. You will soon find comfort within you. When you do, others will begin to notice a difference in you. They will perk up. They will be intrigued. They will wonder about the secret you have that makes you feel so calm, present and well-cared for. You will enjoy sharing what it is that you have—you—but you will no longer feel the urgent need for them to care.

Sincerely,

Libby

 Sometimes the best way to feel that somebody cares is to get in touch with your own caring body. ♡

Too Scared for Friends

Dear Libby,

I have three problems. At school, I'm so anxious I feel sick, and I always come home early. I don't have friends, the work is so hard, I'm too scared to join what the girls are doing. And I can't stop biting my nails.

Scared

Dear Scared,

Anxiety can make anyone feel sick or bite her nails or feel overwhelmed. However, fighting anxiety usually doesn't work. In fact, it makes us feel more anxious, because now we get anxiety about the anxiety. The best thing to do, therefore, is to accept the anxiety, and then find a way to increase comfort and relaxation. This means feeling two emotions at once: anxiety and as much calmness as you can. Try it, and see if you can find a way for the two to coexist peacefully, like twins in a cradle.

Once you feel a bit calmer, you will get a better sense of what care you need. Sometimes the best way to care for yourself is to ask for help. As wonderful it is to be self-reliant and figure things out for ourselves, we need to balance that with the ability to reach out when that is what we need.

Many people tend to hide their needs from others. But the inability to ask for and accept help and guidance comes from fear that something is wrong with us. Asking for help is not a weakness; it's a strength. There are some needs that can be met only through interaction with a person you trust: a parent, teacher, or school counselor may be a good place to start. Knowing how to recognize those needs and asking the appropriate person for help is an act of care.

Sincerely,

Libby

 Speaking to someone you trust to help you out, to listen to what's in your heart, and offer you hope, comfort and guidance is an act of caring for yourself.

Reaching Out for Help
When the Road Gets Rough

Pain is not a weakness. It's a signal. Your mind and body are trying to communicate something it doesn't like. If there is something that's been bothering you for a while, and it keeps you from living your life with joy and hope, it's time to put your discomfort aside, open up and get the help you need. Regardless of what's troubling you, speaking to a reliable adult about it will give you a sense of relief. Think about all the adults in your life, check in with yourself and see who resonates with you and feels safe for you to open up.

If you're embarrassed: It can help if you share your feelings about that too. You can start your conversation by saying something like, "I'm embarrassed about something and find it hard to talk about it." A caring and understanding adult will put you at ease and help you feel safe enough to talk about uncomfortable issues.

Practice how you will say it. Taking the time to collect your thoughts before and thinking about what you want to accomplish, may add comfort and make it easier to express yourself. Sometimes practicing in front of a mirror, or with a friend, or just saying it out loud to yourself, can give you the extra courage.

Try using the written word. Some people find that jotting down their thoughts brings clarity and peacefulness. Sharing what you've put down on paper means you won't have to actually speak about something more than you feel comfortable sharing.

Bring along a support if that helps. Having your best friend with you may help you open up. They can also fill in any information gaps, especially when intense feelings take over.

~~~~~~

Stopping a Friend's Habit

Dear Libby,

My friend daydreams all the time. I really want to help her stop this habit, I just don't know how, and I don't want to hurt her feelings. It gets very annoying.

Annoyed Friend, age 14

Dear Annoyed Friend,

If your friend wants to stop daydreaming, then by all means let her know you're there for her. But don't embark on a mission to fix her. This is not your responsibility. Guess what? She may love her daydreams. A mind that can daydream is a fabulous gift. A wandering mind travels through different parts of our brains and collects bits of information which it can then connect to discover new and creative ideas.

If you feel annoyed by something your friend does, it's not your friend who needs help; it's you. You may want to help her stop certain habits, and maybe you're the one who can benefit from stopping certain habits (like trying to abolish daydreaming).

What is it about her daydreaming that annoys you? Is it because you feel ignored, lonely, or unimportant? Does it get annoying because you feel bored and you want more of her company and attention? Good conversations with a friend can be lots of fun and stimulating for the mind, but two friends can feel very relaxed when they sit together in comfortable silence. If this is not how you feel, then maybe instead of helping your friend, you might help yourself and explore how to find comfort in the quiet stillness of life and indulge in a bit of daydreaming yourself.

Daydreaming offers many benefits. To start with, it allows you to more empathetic, open-minded, and understanding. Your imagination can help you feel someone else's situation and sense what they're experiencing. Daydreaming is also a great way to help you create a vision of something you would like to achieve. Plus, putting your mind on neutral and allowing it to wander a bit helps lower stress and is good for your health. In fact, while you daydream, your brain's problem-solving network is actually more active than when you're focused on doing things.

In the box below, you can find some tips to help you engage with stillness in a mindful way. You can try them when you're alone or with your friend.

Sincerely,

Libby

 Let go of taking care of your friends—they know just how to take care of themselves. Instead, give care to yourself and others.

Daydreaming Can Enrich Your Life

Experiment these stillness workouts anytime you want to give yourself some extra TLC:

Happy Memories: Try to close your eyes and remember a time you felt calm and joyful. Maybe you learned something new and felt the thrill of success. Maybe you did an act of kindness for someone. Maybe someone was kind to you or was really happy to see you. Bring that moment to mind. What were you doing? Let yourself breathe, explore, and relax even as your mind floats from one memory to another. You may begin with your success, wander to thoughts about your favorite pet, jump into your grandmother's arms, and keep going.

Notice how you feel when you remember these pleasant memories.

Go to Sleep Smiling: Right before going to sleep, ask your mind to wonder about the day and recall five things you feel grateful for. Things like the warm sun on your face, an interesting conversation you had with someone, or even a special event you're looking forward to. Spend two or three minutes thinking about the things you appreciate.

Pay attention to how this makes you feel. Does it make you feel heavy or light? Impatient or more relaxed? Just notice without judging.

Listen to the Silence: Sit down and take three slow breaths. Feel each breath from start to finish and be curious about it. How does the air feel as it flows in and out of your nose? Is it cool or warm when it touches the tip of your nose? What does your belly do when you breathe? Does it move up or down, expand or contract? Now enlarge your attention to the environment around you. Can you hear the sound of a car outside, a clock ticking, the refrigerator humming? What does it feel like to listen in stillness?

Notice how listening to your breath and the silence around you makes you feel. Can you sense the stillness?

~~~~~~

Too Sensitive

Dear Libby,

I have a problem. I'm very sensitive. People always tell me to stop being "so sensitive" and not take everything so seriously. I can't handle criticism, and I cry when someone says something mean to me. How can I toughen up?

Sensitive

Dear Sensitive,

Some of the most sensitive people are also the strongest. Sensitive people have a unique ability to meet stress and difficult situations with inner strength. They don't just survive challenges, they thrive and learn from every experience. They do that, not by ignoring their feelings, but by accepting them and using them to their benefit. With time and practice, they develop their skills to face rather than push away the pain or discomfort that comes their way.

Sensitivity is a heightened ability to pick up on sensory information. Like a delicate microphone that detects subtle sounds, sensitive people feel more strongly the sensations in their body. They also detect subtle cues from their environment such as the weather, sounds, smells, and other people's emotions.

Since sensitive people feel deeply, they can easily become overwhelmed. This makes them believe they're not as tough as everyone else—that they're too soft or weak and need someone else to be in charge. But the ability to feel their sensations carries many natural gifts, like creativity, empathy and an ability to live with joy and gratitude. In fact, it's their very sensitivity that guides them to develop skills that help them be in charge of their own feelings and use it for the good of the world.

When we want to get rid of our discomfort quickly, we often attack ourselves by saying things like, "Stupid tears, stupid fear. Why do they have to come right now? What's wrong with me? I shouldn't be so sensitive!" Instead, try to take some time to explore the sensations in your body and to engage with them, by observing them. "Hmmm, I feel uneasy butterflies in my stomach and my eyes burning with tears right now, and that is okay. I can have my feelings and my tears can be there."

When you do that, you are kind to yourself. You're giving your mind and body a message that you care, and that it's okay to be you and feel what's really there. You can face any discomfort and sense your breath at the same time. If you succeed at facing an unwanted reality and continue to follow and slow your breath, you will gradually feel calmer. The discomfort might not diminish right away, but you will feel better, more real, more alive. As you connect to your own sensations and emotions, you gradually connect with everything around you—your friends, the birds, the flowers, and life itself.

Sometimes sensitive people feel different and alone, but the truth is, many people know what it's like to be you. Spending time with other sensitive people who are thriving and living with vitality, can be comforting and help you feel understood. Together, you can encourage each other to value the special qualities of sensitivity and cherish it as your gift.

Sincerely,

Libby

Sensitivity is a heightened ability to pick up on sensory information. ♡

~~~~~~~~~~~~~~~~~~~~~~~~~~~~~~~~

She Offends Us

Dear Libby,

My friend and I have a classmate we're both friendly with but who often does and says things that offends us and others. She's easily hurt but doesn't realize when she hurts others. She imagines everyone is against her and tells anyone willing to listen. She doesn't allow the one of us who's closer to her to make other friends. She lacks other basic social skills also. We feel these problems need to be taken care of before school starts, so please reply as soon as possible. Thank you very much.

Two Desperate Friends

Dear Two Desperate Friends,

Hurt people hurt people. Because of their pain, people who are hurting inside misinterpret ordinary words to mean something negative toward them. Their inner pain is so raw that they're extremely sensitive, often absorbed in their own pain and unaware that they're hurting others. Naturally, when this distances others, they don't understand why no one is there for them.

As you've discovered, friendships are two-sided. We have a responsibility to treat others and ourselves with respect. Whether we find a comment stinging and hurtful, or just clueless and annoying, our responsibility lies in how we choose to respond—and that always includes kindness. With practice, we can learn to protect ourselves and avoid taking insensitive words too much to heart. While it's normal to feel hurt and angry, forgiving someone is an act of self-care more than it is about caring for others (except in the case of bullying, which is best addressed by a professional). Holding on to resentment hurts you most.

In your letter you mention that these problems need to be taken care of before school starts, which seems to imply that somebody "out there" should take care of the problem. In this case, you can rely on your own maturity and wisdom and your ability to look beyond the surface—to see this girl for who she is: a person with a heart, with feelings, with pain. With that fuller perspective, you can rise above your own sensitivities and respond with kindness. Discover the joy of respecting others for who they are, of honoring another person's dignity, of your power to make someone's face glow with the feeling of acceptance. "When you are good to others, you are best to yourself." (Benjamin Franklin)

Sincerely,

Libby

 The ability to care for yourself is the ability to care for others.

~~~~~~

Pushing Away My Help

Dear Libby,

I have a friend who's so shy. I'm trying to help her self-esteem, but she keeps pushing me away. My goal is to get her to be in the end-of-year play, but I don't think I'll be able to do that. How can I help her?

A Caring Friend

Dear Caring Friend,

If your friend wants to be in the end-of-year play, then you can let her know that you will support her to follow her dreams, but this is a choice she will make, not you. What gives you the idea that you need to help her? If your friend has no interest in your help, then maybe it's time to step back and enjoy her for who she is. Self-esteem, by its very definition, means esteem from the self, from within, and not from others. So, you're right; you will not be able to achieve this goal. You cannot control another's interests or goals, but you can set your own goals. How about replacing this goal with something far more doable, like caring for yourself?

When we *take care* of our friends, it's not the same as when we *give care*. Taking care may be a way to take control or take charge of someone's life and deciding what's best for them. This makes you feel stressed and frustrated. Giving care feels more loving. It is energizing and uplifting. It has the other person's best interests at heart. It shows trust in their ability to take care of themselves. Taking care is about you, giving care is about the other person.

Sometimes the impulse to take care of others comes from feeling a void or a lack of care yourself. Taking care of other people is a way to get care for yourself when they appreciate and admire you in return. The more we can *give* care, the less care we need to *take* from others—and the happier our friendships can be.

Once you learn to care for yourself, the urgency you feel to take care of someone else will decrease. You will know how to sense your own needs and explore ways to meet them. You will then truly give of yourself to others for the sake of giving not taking, acknowledging that everyone can have the dreams and goals of their own choice.

Sincerely,

Libby

 Your ability to care for yourself will help you give care instead of take care.

People Don't Like Me

Dear Libby,

I have a problem. People don't like me (at least kids don't). They call me names. I try to ignore them but I can't. I call them names back, even though I know that's not nice. What should I do?

Love,

Not Liked

Dear Not Liked,

It's normal to get upset and want to hurt back when someone hurts you. This is just what the one hurting you is aiming for, and it will only make matters worse. See if you can act brave even if you don't feel that way. Assume an air of confidence. Relax your body (take a few deep breaths) and assert yourself by saying once (more than once is counter-effective), something like, "Don't talk to me like that." Or, "I want you to stop right now."

Kids don't really mean it when they say, "I don't like you." To really mean it they would have to know you first and then decide that they don't like what they see. The important thing is that we like and respect ourselves. Remember that you are a precious living being here on this world with a special mission to fulfill. You are the only one in this world who can accomplish your specific role in the best way possible with the tools you have been given. Discover your beautiful qualities and learn to cherish them.

When you respect yourself two things will happen:

1. You will feel it is beneath your dignity to react by giving it back at them, and so you will be able to better resist this impulse. This in turn will help you feel better about yourself. *Self-control breeds self-respect.*

2. Others will sense that you have respect for yourself and will respect you too! We first need to love and appreciate ourselves in order for others to respect us.

Sincerely,

Libby

 If you can stay calm and caring to yourself as best as you can, others will take their cues from you.

Did She Just Hurt Me?

Dear Libby,

I would be very happy if you could help me with a few problems that have been bothering me for a quite a while now.

I'm extremely sensitive, especially with friends. The tiniest comment goes straight to my heart and makes me feel bad. When a friend tells me a simple statement or something that's meant to be a joke, I start thinking deeper into it, for example, what did she really mean to say with it? Did she want to hurt me, etc.?

My friends say that if someone feels hurt by her friend's words it's her own problem and means she's lacking self-confidence. Is this true?

Troubled

Dear Troubled,

You seem to be very in touch with your feelings, and that is wonderful. If you feel hurt by others then you probably were hurt. Trust your feelings; feelings are very real. As for sensitivity, that's a beautiful quality that helps you tune into the needs of yourself and others with understanding and empathy. Sensitive people also appreciate the finer, more delicate aspects of life.

That said, sometimes we're already experiencing so much discomfort that even the smallest comment is painful, even when your friends didn't mean to hurt you. It's like when a person's arm is sunburned and the slightest tap feels painful to the touch.

We may not be able to control life's circumstances or how people talk to us, but with practice we can manage our responses. Compassion in the face of unkind words is a very effective response. That's not to say that you need to deny or ignore your feelings. You can allow yourself to feel what comes up for you; simply say to yourself, "This hurts," and breathe.

Acknowledging your feelings is an act of care. Often, we'd rather not face the fact that we're hurt; we want to let it go without letting it get to us. The truth is that most of the time discomfort or hurt feelings is not something we can avoid or get rid of, but we can always get through them.

Once you feel your own care, you will feel stronger. You'll be able to see unkindness for what it really is—an instinctive reaction from a wounded human being who feels tiny and probably threatened. Strong people are sensitive and kind.

Sincerely,

Libby

 Acknowledging your feelings is an act of care.

~~~~~~

Embarrassing Problem

Dear Libby,

I have a very embarrassing problem. I stutter and girls laugh at me in class. Please help me quickly.

Laughed At

Dear Laughed At,

Stuttering can be a real challenge. Anything that makes us feel different, tends to make us feel lonely. Yet, you're not alone. There are millions of people in the world who stutter.

Many people don't know or understand much about stuttering. Try to learn more about the subject so that you can understand it better and help others understand it as well.

Every time you talk, your brain, lungs, vocal cords, lips, tongue, and teeth work together in a specific pattern. Sometimes, when there's a lot of tension in the muscles that help you talk, stuttering results. When your speech muscles fail to do what you want them to do, you feel out of control and frustrated. However, there are many tips and techniques that you can learn to help you feel more in control and make it easier for you to talk. Speak to your parents about finding a speech therapist who can help you. There are a variety of successful approaches for treating stuttering.

Sometimes, perhaps without even realizing it, classmates and friends tease others for their differences in order to make themselves feel better. They work under the misconception that if they make others feel bad, they'll feel better about themselves. Of course, this isn't true. No one feels better by hurting others. Other times, people laugh at us because they feel uncomfortable and nervous about how to react. Often, the best way to deal with this is to let your classmates know that you're not bothered by your stuttering. When you feel comfortable with yourself, others will feel more comfortable around you and will not laugh out of nervous tension.

You have infinite and intrinsic worth just for being you.

Sincerely,

Libby

 Care about the words you say, not just the way you say them. Be patient with yourself and know that the words will come.

Final Thoughts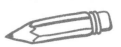

Your body is designed to support you to feel energized, animated, alive, and joyful. Your brain has a whole pharmacy of natural remedies to help you manage pain, calm stress, and soothe sadness. It is open twenty-four seven and you can access your own supply of care anytime you want.

Nourish Yourself:
- Walking, dancing, and running are all essential forms of nourishment. Physical activity activates your feel-good hormones. Make exercise a simple, daily habit. It's fun and rewarding.
- Notice which friendships add joy to your life and which drain you of energy.

- Pay attention to your emotional wellbeing. Your body responds to the way you think, feel and act.
- Care about your body's messages, like tummy aches, the inability to sleep, or a constant feeling of tiredness; they tell you that something isn't right.
- In your journal write a list of five things you need in order to feel cared for and valued. Allow yourself to be authentic. Your list might include things like:

  1. I need to feel appreciated
  2. I need to be told that I'm cute
  3. I need _____
  4. I need _____
  5. I need _____

Now, close your eyes and, one statement at a time, grant yourself each item on your list by speaking it to yourself silently or out loud. For example:

- I need to feel appreciated: *I appreciate myself.*
- I need to be told that I'm cute: *I acknowledge that I'm cute.*

~~~~~~

Make It Yours

Write a letter to yourself, written to you, by your ideal best friend. When you're done, re-read your letter and allow yourself to imagine these words being spoken to you with great kindness and care. Allow your heart to open and receive the sweet sentiments that you've written.

COMFORT

Chapter 3:

Comfort Yourself

Don't escape your discomfort, add comfort to face, contain, understand, and outgrow it.

—GINO GROSS

*L*ife is movement and movement is life. Without movement, there is no life. If we were to ask ourselves how we move, we would find that there are two basic ways. We're either moving away from pain or toward pleasure. And in between we pause. Of course, even when we pause, there is a subtle movement. Even in stillness there is an underlying motion, a harmony, a rhythm, a flow, like the quiet ripples on the surface of the lake.

If we were to observe how we usually move, we would probably find that we constantly move away from pain. Much of our lives, most people, day after day, just keep moving away. We don't want to feel pain. And while pleasure is great, and we want that, what we want more is to avoid pain.

If a tiger were running after you, or you saw a basket holding all your dreams—tickets to Disneyland, the prettiest jewelry, bundles of cash, or whatever your heart desires, which one would get you to act the quickest? Well, duh, the tiger of course. But why?

Any time our survival instinct to avoid pain is triggered, everything else shuts down. The reflex to keep you out of harm's way overrides just about every other desire in that moment. Whenever it senses danger, your instinct goes to war, mobilizing your entire defense force to escape the enemy: it pumps adrenaline and cortisol into your bloodstream, speeds up your heartbeat, pushes blood to your muscles, widens small airways in your lungs, and sends extra oxygen to your brain to keep you alert and your senses sharp.

The energy of your survival mechanism charges through your body like electrical impulses urging you to move, sometimes even before you had a chance to fully process what is happening. That's why you can move your hands away from fire faster than your mind knows something is hot, because your mind will ensure you bypass thoughts or judgments that slow you down. Eventually, you become aware of what's going on, but your mind made sure, that your body moved first—reflexively and instinctively.

If you pay attention, you can actually feel the survival activity in your body, such as your muscles tightening, your heart racing, or your arms tingling. Your body's security system creates an energy of movement in your body. In the case of imminent threat, it urges you to move away giving you the superpowers to jump off a flying bike or climb a tree when a tsunami hits.

But there's a problem. The security system makes mistakes. When it comes to pain and danger, our security system follows the rule of better safe than sorry, act first think later, and when in doubt, run. This system works fast and doesn't look for accuracy, which is why it's based on simple associations, not deliberate consideration and thought. Such slower thinking, in times of real danger can cost us our lives. But this fast thinking security system can easily trigger false alarms and drive movement without thinking.

That's why we so often do or say things we immediately regret. Because while the survival instinct is there to protect you, it's not striving to be wise. It's like a robot that does its job faithfully: it looks out for danger. When it perceives danger, or even what looks like danger, it instantly blasts at full volume, in a non-stop repetition, "NO. NO. NO. NO. I don't want this!"

So, say you're talking with a friend and there's a lull in the conversation, and an inner voice whispers to you that you're not good enough, or maybe you're not popular enough and you'll be rejected.

Before you know it, your security system has gone into full gear. Your heartbeat quickens, your knees feel a bit wobbly, maybe you blush or feel slightly dizzy, your tummy feels tight, and your mind races, "What should I say? I shouldn't have said that. What is she thinking? Oh my goodness, is everyone looking at me? Did I do something stupid? Will I do something stupid?"

You've become gripped by fear, you're not thinking straight and have no access to wisdom—all in the name of survival. What would best suit this situation? Not movement *away*, driven by fear, but movement *toward*, inspired by choice. What this friendship now needs, is not a powerful "No," but a vision of "Yes," not a quick-fix solution to get rid of discomfort, but a calm, thoughtful approach to realign the relationship.

But you see, your security system doesn't really tell you what to say yes to or how to be calm and comfortable or how to live with joy and vitality or how to grow friendships. Because while all it wants is to survive, it doesn't understand living. It simply does its job, robotically, preparing you to combat or escape potential danger.

So, what can you do when your survival system has been mistakenly activated, but your living system is the best way forward? One very important rule is that you can't fight your security system or the survival instinct. It always fights back. And it wins every time. Try it. If you feel angry (a defense movement of attack) tell yourself not to get angry. If you feel fear, tell yourself not to be afraid. If you blush, tell your face not to blush. Get rid of it. Quickly, please. Does it work? Not very well. It just adds fuel to the flames. In the effort to push away the pain, you inadvertently end up creating more pain, a survival reflex on top of a survival reflex. You have double-trouble. So now what?

Well, you can ignore it. You know, pretend it's not there, deny it, stuff it in the back of your mind, or distract yourself with heaps of ice cream and movies and shopping trips. Lots of people do that. But those are very short-term strategies that create long-term problems.

Using pleasure to cover up pain causes more damage than good. There is another way.

Instead of trying to get rid of the pain, you can *add* comfort. The ability to comfort yourself is a skill any of us can learn. You practice, and little by little, you find it gets easier to accomplish.

Once you create within yourself a comfortable enough space for comfort and pain to coexist. You no longer feel the same urgency to act. You can resist moving impulsively until you know how to move wisely. This ability to pause, to be still, depends on how much you can bear. It depends on your pain threshold, which is something you can increase through practice. While it might be hard at the beginning, and it might feel like a long dark tunnel, it is really worth investing in. When you learn to bear and contain all that uncomfortable survival energy surging through your body, you come out on the other side of the tunnel, into the light—you enter the *land of the living*.

In the land of the living we act with intention and not compulsion, we move with flow, with dignity and beauty and grace.

So, is our security system completely wrong, or does it have a point when it activates its full power? The surprising answer is, our security system is rarely wrong in identifying issues and concerns that need addressing, but it is very often mistaken about how to address and fix them. To be alerted or warned by our security system about what we dislike and what doesn't work for us, is crucial, but driving us to run away or attack is often going too far. Through adding comfort, by calming ourselves down, we can reduce our survival instinct, our fight-or-flight response, until it becomes a subtler signal we can, and should, carefully listen to. Our pains and dislikes, should be calmly and wisely addressed with our living and growing system. Rather than finding an escape route from pain, our adding of comfort helps us stand still and face the discomfort with courage.

Life Seems to Be Hard

Dear Libby,

I keep worrying about the future. I enjoy life, thankfully, and know that there's lots of happiness in life, but the older I get, I keep seeing more and more problems, troubles and worries. The younger I was, the more friends I had; the older I get, I see that relationships become more and more complicated. Life seems to be hard. How will I manage? I try to strengthen my trust and faith, but I still worry. What should I do? Please help me fast because these problems really trouble me very much.

Troubled

Dear Troubled,

On the canvas of life, we observe sunrise and sunset, mountains and valleys, joy and pain. Collectively, they represent reality. Joyful living is only possible when we open ourselves up to each experience life offers.

Young children approach life with spontaneity and awe, full of wonder and joy. They're curious about why the sky is blue or where rain comes from, and how the next minute will unfold in this miraculous world. Between childhood and adulthood, something happens.

As we start to become burdened with responsibilities, experience doubt over our decisions, or feel saddened by things that happen, we no longer feel comfortable with surprises. We want to know what will happen next. We crave certainty and hold on to any illusion that gives us a sense of control. We no longer allow the magic of life to unfold.

It is our reluctance to accept the fluid nature of life, the uncertainties, the ups and downs, the chaos and the delights, which causes distress. We stop experiencing the full array of choices our journey offers us. We like to think we know how things ought to be and feel that life should be generally good.

The logical mind attaches judgments to the challenges we encounter in life and label them as troubles or pleasures. It asks, how can this be happening to me? Wisdom, conversely, seeks to learn from each experience. It asks, how can this be good for me? It knows that life happens just the way it is supposed to happen, the unpredictable, the joyful, the sad, the miracles, and tragedies all rolled up into one incredibly short experience. And often, the very things that seem tragic are blessings in disguise.

But challenges have a hypnotic power. Our minds tend to zoom into the misfortunes of life and make them appear larger-than-life. What we need to do is adjust the lens, and reclaim the full, panoramic view of life. That's not an easy task, because worry and fear keep us transfixed. Imagine that you hear an unfamiliar sound outside your door. You look out through the peephole but you don't see much. So you stay there, rooted to the spot, eyes glued to the tiny door viewer. Fear can do that to us.

The more frightened and worried we become, the more our focus remains narrow. The question is, how can we zoom out again? We can learn to manage, not the circumstances, but our attention to the circumstances. Challenges are there, and we do our best to overcome them. But they shouldn't seize all of our attention. Keep your eyes on the prize—a life lived with vitality, joy and wisdom—and the distresses of life will be easier to handle. "The purpose of life, after all," Eleanor Roosevelt said, "is to live it, to taste, experience to the utmost, to reach out eagerly and without fear for newer and richer experiences."

Take charge of your own attention. Look for the sun twice as much as you see the clouds. Those truisms about making lemonades when life gives you lemons and seeing the glass half-full doesn't mean that we need to be blind to the realities of life. But to get the most out of life, we need to learn to allocate our attention effectively. Attention, after all, is a precious resource. We only have so much of it.

Pay attention to the life that beats inside you. Discover the activities that feel meaningful to you and make you come alive with a sense of purpose and joy. Who are you? What do you stand for? What are your values? What is most important to you to live a fully authentic life? Maybe it's serving children with special needs; maybe it's sending packages or cards to deployed troops, veterans or wounded soldiers; maybe it's teaching computer skills at a senior center, or volunteering to tutor.

When you share with others that which is alive in you, your talents, your abilities, your interests, not only do you enhance another person's life, but you enrich your own.

Sincerely,

Libby

 When you express your aliveness, you can show up and be present to the small blessings that happen every day.

What to Say or Ask
Yourself to Add Comfort

"I am here; you are safe." Fear has a way of making things look worse and feel scarier, but self-soothing is a wonderful skill to practice.

"Tell me about it." Invite your discomfort to a 10–15 minute "play date" to speak. Give it a space to tell you about itself. You don't need to fix it or change anything. Just be there for it and listen.

"Who or what can make it worse?" If you can identify what triggers this discomfort, you can bring it down to size. It can help you convince your mind that whatever it fears is not actually dangerous.

"It's scary AND . . ." Acknowledge your fear and add something. After the word "and" you can add phrases like, "You are safe," or "You've had that fear before and you calmed it down," or "I'm still breathing."

"What do you feel like doing?" Your discomfort is an impulse to run or chase or attack. It wants to move. Knowing how it wants to move, doesn't mean that you'll enact that movement, but it will help you slow down the motion inside your body.

"I know, but not now." You say this gently. When the discomfort feels that it has a soothing inner guide, it can pause and calm down. It learns to trust you, even if it doesn't yet see a way out.

"What do you need from me?" Show it that you care. Maybe it would like a hot chocolate or some music or just to rest.

"This discomfort will pass." All feelings pass eventually. When feelings are intense, they can feel like they will never end, you won't make it through, or it's too hard. And that's normal and okay.

Fear looks different for everyone. Some of these strategies will work better for you than others. You are the best expert on yourself. Play with them, and eventually, you will find what helps you send a calm and comforting message to your mind.

Controlling Emotions

Dear Libby,

I have a problem. Sometimes I don't know how to control my emotions, and I yell and scream. A lot of times I tell myself: Today you're not going to yell. You're going to change. An amazing teacher once told me that she thinks I'm a bit intense. I even asked my friend to tell me if she thinks so, and she said . . . "Yes!" I've realized that I am intense, and I want to stop.

I cry very easily too. (Of course, not in school!!!)

Please give me some ideas how to:

1. *control my emotions*

2. *calm myself down when I want to yell (I've tried counting to ten, but it didn't really work)*

3. *stop being intense*

4. *not cry so easily*

Wants to Control Her Emotions

Dear Wants to Control Her Emotions,

Emotions are an essential part of life. They are neither mystical nor mysterious but are tangible energies in the body. They can be felt as a force in you that drives motion or an inner calmness that encourages rest. We can learn to manage these energies, not by ignoring them or fighting them, but by understanding and coordinating them.

People who have learned to manage the energies in their bodies, instead of allowing these energies to manage them, are called *emotionally intelligent*. Anyone can learn to be emotionally intelligent and manage their energy of motion (*e-motion*) properly.

Here are some tips to get you started:

Gather a support system. Ask your parents or your friends to help and encourage you. Find a role model who's good at this, like a teacher or mentor who can help you process and deal with the intense or stormy movement energies in your body in a productive way.

Set little goals for yourself. Big goals are reached by taking small steps, one at a time. Achieving little changes help you experience some of the benefits of your goal while building momentum to keep you going. Start with exploring five different ways to add calm energy to your body when you're feeling anger, fear, or pain. Even just wondering about helpful ideas can be a little goal in itself. Your next goal can be to try out one of those ideas. And so on.

Celebrate small successes. If you can manage to reduce the number of times you resist enacting your motion energy, enjoy that. If you bring your yelling down from ten times a day to three, treat yourself. Celebrate even when you can manage to refrain from yelling at least once a day, or once in two days. Each triumph is a stepping-stone.

Plan for setbacks. Any time we choose to change, there will be challenging moments. But if you prepare yourself in advance for setbacks, you'll know how to respond when they happen. Say you have an action plan to take five deep breaths whenever you feel intense emotions surging through your body. Then, when someone "steps on your toes," you're ready to manage your emotions.

Sincerely,

Libby

 Learning to manage our emotions is a process. Aiming for small changes helps build momentum and reaps some of the benefits along the way.

Will They Treat Me Differently?

Dear Libby,

I'm really scared to go to sleep away camp, because I have scoliosis, and I wear a back brace. In truth, I am a social person. I have the ability to make a lot of friends. I'm afraid though that my bunkmates will treat me differently and that, because of my problem, I will be shy and embarrassed to make new friends. I'm also worried that people who don't know about my back brace will ask me what's sticking out, and I will be way too embarrassed to answer them. Please, please X 100 help me enjoy camp without feeling embarrassed.

Scared to Go to Camp

Dear Scared to Go to Camp,

Your courage to face your fears and go to camp even while concerned about how your back brace will be seen by others, is an inspiration for all of us. Often people who find themselves a bit outside the norm end up being the ones helping the norm grow. They are the visionaries and innovators who bring something new and refreshing to the world.

Meeting new people and undertaking new experiences can feel terrifying if you focus on other people's reactions but can be very satisfying if you focus on your own actions. You have the ability to make a lot of friends, and you know that. This means that you know how to be kind and empathetic to others. Hold on to that. It will help you consider other people's intrusive questions as clues to their inner discomfort. They may be uneasy themselves about your brace due to a lack of experience, not a lack of acceptance. Asking questions may be a way of trying to connect with you.

You're scared that you'll be embarrassed, but you needn't be; if you remember all that is unique and special and miraculous about you, you can enjoy camp. Don't let questions keep you from having a good time. If they can ask whatever they want, you can answer whatever you want, such as, "Ask me some other questions because lots of people ask me this all the time, and I'm already bored of that one." You can just be straight-forward and say, "I don't feel so comfortable talking about that, can we talk about something else?" You'll say it a couple of times and everybody will stop. And you'll feel good knowing that you're in charge of how you choose to answer anybody.

See yourself and hold on to who you are. Camp is your opportunity to take what makes you different, to make a difference. You are one of those special individuals who can see beyond outer appearances into inner value.

Sincerely,

Libby

 Allow your disability to open your eyes to your true abilities. It's not about your *disability*, but your *different*-ability.

~~~~~~

Personal Secrets or Friend?

Dear Libby,

My friend always bugs me to tell her my secrets and ignores me or is mean to me if I don't. Now I found out that this girl I thought was my friend was telling people my secrets. I want to be her friend, but I'm not her friend anymore, and I'm very lonely. I realized I don't even have one true friend. Can you tell me how I could make friends?

Lonely Girl

Dear Lonely Girl,

You may be alone, and loneliness may be tough, but it can also be valuable and replenishing. You are probably asking yourself, "How much do we have to give up for friends, and when is it so much that it's no longer a friendship?" Or, "How can I have friends if I want to respect my privacy?" Perhaps you're realizing, *hmm, if I don't tell my secrets, then I don't have friends.*

This is an opportunity for you to spend time with yourself, to get to know yourself, and evaluate the price you're prepared to pay for a friendship.

Every friendship requires sacrifice, but sometimes the sacrifice is so big that the friendship is not worth the price. While you don't want to be alone, you don't want to give up on your privacy. You have a right to expect your privacy to be respected. Allowing your friend to spread private information, because otherwise you'll feel lonely, is not the price you're prepared to pay for this friendship.

In a true friendship we can talk about the sacrifices that each of us make. If it feels right for you, you may want to check with your friend about what happened, and to see if there still is a possibility for it to be a friendship or if it's something else. Such a conversation may end up with her asking forgiveness, and no longer revealing your secrets, or it may end up with you once again feeling that you must make a decision between guarding your secrets and keeping your friend.

Loneliness, or "alone time" may feel rough. It's the discomfort that often creates a push and pull effect, like a conflict tugging in two different directions. You want, and you don't want. You want a friend but you don't want to give up on your privacy. You don't want to be alone, but you only want to have a true friend.

This inner struggle can make you feel very uneasy, even physically so. If you pay attention, you can actually feel all the movement energy somewhere in your body. Nobody likes to feel that. We usually look for the quickest exit from which to escape that. We can't bear the discomfort of holding on to our personal secrets, and so we tell them against our better judgment.

But you're not doing that.

You're prepared to wait. To be lonely for a while. That is a wise, mature decision.

Quick, fast, rash actions lack wisdom. They sees only one or two options. Slowing down requires the ability to bear some discomfort without rushing to get rid of it, but it gives you access to a wider range of choices. Then maybe you can have both: keep your privacy and not be lonely. By creating a space for discomfort and comfort to coexist you gain wisdom and the freedom to choose a friend that feels right for you.

Sincerely,

Libby

Every friendship requires sacrifice, but sometimes the sacrifice is so big that it's no longer a friendship. ♡

Sometimes She Ignores Me

Dear Libby,

I have a friend who sometimes ignores me. I don't want to leave her, because I don't have any other friends. Please help me fast. I can't take it anymore.

Love,

Can't Take It Anymore

Dear Can't Take It Anymore,

Feeling alone and without friends can be very uncomfortable. Since nobody likes to feel discomfort, we usually try to avoid or escape it in any way possible, even if it means holding on to a friend who is ignoring us.

Strangely enough, the more you run from the discomfort, the more it seems to follow you.

Think of this scene: A small rock is lying on the street. Many people pass it by. They step on it, kick it slightly into the air, toss it to the side. Mostly, nobody pays it too much attention. Now imagine a three-year-old girl learning how to ride her first bike. Her hands grip the handlebars, she leans over and keeps her eyes focused on the floor. She notices the rock. It becomes huge in her mind. The people on the street disappear, the surroundings vanish, as she keeps her eyes on the rock for fear of bumping into it. It's just a pebble. But because of the fear, it feels so big, and she wishes to avoid it at all costs. She tries to peddle her bike away from it. Yet, she is hypnotized by that pebble, drawn to it, and finally, knocks into it. She collides with the very things she wanted most to avoid.

How does this happen?

When we're afraid of facing our fears, they seem to have more power over us. The more we try to avoid pain, the more we become riveted to it, often without realizing it. Your friend is causing you pain by ignoring you yet, you're gripped by the thought that you don't want to leave her. What are you really trying to avoid? Not having friends? Being alone? True, maybe sometimes she doesn't ignore you, and you have fun together, but are you then becoming so absorbed in her that you cannot go and make other friends at the same time?

When you know how to comfort yourself, you're not dependent on what a friend does or doesn't do. You always have your own friendship. If a friend ignores you because she's busy or hanging out with someone else, you're happy to find other friends. But, if the reason you have a friend is because you wish to avoid the pain of being alone, then you don't have a friend, and your friend is not ignoring you, because you were never friends to begin with. You're just holding on to her like a drowning person holds on to a floating board, so that you absolutely don't end up alone.

Fear of loneliness can be so big, like a pebble to a little girl riding her first bike. It's so frightening, you run from this very idea. What would it take if instead, you to turn and face loneliness? Would it hurt? Maybe. But not as bad as it hurts now.

Pain or discomfort is never as awful as we imagine it to be. And if you stop running from it, you free up all that energy to get to know yourself better. You can take time to reflect about your likes and dislikes, your opinions about things happening. What is your favorite song? Who do you admire? What do you want to learn about? There's a whole world of information waiting for you inside yourself. You can have such a good time with learning about yourself that other girls will be curious and want to know what you have that makes life so fun for you.

Sincerely,

Libby

 The more you run away from discomfort, the more it seems to pursue you.

Very Sensitive

Dear Libby,

I'm very sensitive. I can't help myself. I try to be toughen up and be strong, but it doesn't help. I just cry.

Sensitive

Dear Sensitive,

Sensitivity is an innate quality and a highly developed ability to experience the flow of sensory input. This allows you to see the world in more vivid colors, sounds, smell, taste, and touch. Sensitive people have rich inner lives with a deep appreciation for beauty. They are highly creative, imaginative, and caring. With sensitivity you might be able to sense very deeply what other people feel. You hear not just the words people say, but you also catch on to subtleties in gesture and tone. This sensitivity can help you enjoy the more delicate and finer things in life like art or music.

Sensitivity is a great gift, but it's sometimes also a burden. Maybe it's a blessing in disguise. Sometimes we need to be prepared to pay the price of crying for the benefit of sensitivity.

Perhaps you don't need to be tough, but soft and strong. Not all of us are like the oak tree, some of us are like the more pliable trees, able to bend with the wind, so that when you experience a strong gust of sensitivity you are able to stretch with it and then come back.

Maybe instead of trying to run away from your sensitivity, embrace it. Resisting something doesn't make it go away; it always increases discomfort. Instead, add some comfort to your discomforts and the intensity will calm down. Become friends with your sensitivity. By accepting and cherishing your soft and delicate nature, you can be strong.

So, if you're sensitive and you feel like crying, have a good cry. Then listen and understand what your sensitivity is trying to say with the tears. Let your sensitivity be your inner guide.

Sincerely,

Libby

 Sensitivity is a fine quality that helps you be attuned to the beauty in life and the splendor in people.

~~~~~~

Stage Fright

Dear Libby,

I love to sing and I have a beautiful voice. All my close friends say that. But I have stage fright. Whenever I'm on stage, my legs feel like jelly and my voice shakes. If I sing for close family and friends, I'm okay, but on stage, I'm out of control. Please help me fast. I feel like I'm wasting my talent.

Singer

Dear Singer,

Stage fright is a very common form of uneasy feelings that has to do with performing in front of others. It often occurs when we feel like we're being judged or evaluated. This discomfort is felt in different ways for different people. Some people, like you, feel a weakness in their legs and tension in the vocal chords. Others experience icy, frozen fingers, trembling in the legs or arms, queasiness in the stomach, tightness in the chest or throat. Contrast these painful sensations with the ones we feel when we're calm: an expansive, flowing sensation in the chest and tingling in the arms; we feel free, energized, light, safe, firm, and stable.

Since no one likes to feel uncomfortable, and because tense muscles prevent us from performing our best, we tend to try, with all our might, to push those uncomfortable feelings away. It becomes a fight, but when we fight fear, fear usually wins. Instead of feeling better, we end up feeling worse.

The best thing to do is . . . guess what? Stop fighting. I know. It's easier said than done. But if you think about it, how will a tight chest or weak legs that feel like jelly help you sing well? Instead, what you can do is bring more calmness into your body. That means that you shift your focus to calming activities, like paying attention to your breathing, relaxing your chest muscles, and sensing your feet touching the ground. Repeating a mantra can also help, like, "I'm safe. This may be uncomfortable, but I am okay." Instead of running from the fear and from uncomfortable sensations in your body, decide that you'll focus on relaxing your body.

Breathing is something that our bodies do automatically, and not something we usually think about. But paying attention to it offers our body a gentle invitation to slow down our breathing, slow down our thoughts, and gives our brain a message that we're safe. Practice being conscious of your breathing while singing to an audience you feel safe with, like family or friends.

You can also try visualizing yourself singing before an audience. Since our subconscious mind doesn't really differentiate between the real and the imagined, it's likely that your body will activate some of the uncomfortable physical sensations of fear just by visualizing it. That is your opportunity to practice relaxing.

When you do get on stage, plant your feet firmly on the ground, take as much time as you need to relax, and breathe calmly before singing. Stand with poise and confidence, connect with your audience and see them for the people they really are—caring individuals who are rooting for you, who want you to succeed, who want to be treated with the gift of your beautiful voice. It is ultimately about inspiring others and sharing your gifts.

Sincerely,

Libby

Redirecting your attention to your breath is a gentle invitation to slow down your body and your thoughts; it gives your brain a message that you're safe.

Don't Subtract, Add

Five minutes of adding comfort every day can make a big difference:

- Listen to soothing, peaceful music.
- Practice deep breathing.
- Imagine yourself in peaceful, relaxing situations like a peaceful island or secret garden.

Here's how you can learn the difference between tension and discomfort in your body, and softness and comfort:

Tight as a tennis ball. Imagine that you are holding a tennis ball in your hand. Clench your fist and squeeze it as tightly as you can. Now let go. Next, scrunch up your face like you would if someone squirted lemon juice at you. Tighten your forehead, your eyes, nose, lips and tongue. Let go. Soften the muscles in your face. Let it all relax. Try it with your legs. Tighten them, curl up your toes, then soften and let go. Now you can feel the difference in your muscles when they are tense compared to when they are relaxed.

Create a routine. Set aside a regular time to practice adding comfort. Make it a daily habit just like brushing your teeth. Make yourself as comfortable as you can in a warm and relaxed place, like your bed, a comfy chair, or a mat on the floor and practice your calming skills.

Bring it with you. The more you are able to add comfort to your body, the more you can begin to bring this comfort with you in everyday real-life situations. Instead of running from difficult experience, you will be able to focus on softening the muscles in your body and your ability to breath deeply and rhythmically.

Experiment and explore different ways to add comfort in your own way, at your own pace, whenever it feels comfortable for you to do so. With time, you will be able to meet situations in life with comfort and with courage.

I Shout My Feelings

Dear Libby,

I have a hard time expressing the way I feel without shouting. No one wants to listen to me because it's so annoying, but I can't stop! Please help me.

Noisy

Dear Noisy,

The only way to stop doing something is to stop. It's easy to keep doing something you're used to doing, unless you get smart and realize, *Goodness, this way isn't working.*

Like with everything new, it takes practice to get good at it. So don't worry about sometimes forgetting and shouting instead of

99

talking. Just take a minute to pause, reorient yourself, and connect with the comfort in your body. Slowing down your breath and softening your muscles tends to soothe intense emotions sends a calm message to the brain, "Ssshhh," it says, "It's okay, now. I'm safe."

This doesn't mean that you can never feel angry or stressed or have the impulse to shout about something. You can have your feelings, find a way to comfort yourself, and when you're calmer, talk about it in a more grown up way. Here's an extra tip: if you open your mouth, and you find your voice coming out noisy and loud, grab a pen and paper, and express yourself in writing first. After all, you can't really shout and write at the same time! Spill out all your feelings there and this will lessen their intensity, so when you talk you'll express yourself clearly and maturely. The positive results you'll get will motivate you to keep going.

Sincerely,

Libby

 You can gently resist old patterns of behavior to allow better and more mature ones to take their place. ♡

Stressed Out

Dear Libby,

I'm just a stressed-out person, and because of that I get annoyed at my friends very quickly, and then I regret it. My friends and even my parents are always telling me to

try to be calmer, but I can't try. I'm full of
stress. Please help me ASAP.

Stressed Girl

Dear Stressed Girl,

Stress is your body's way of responding to any kind of threat. When you have lots of movement energy rushing around in your body you can physically feel it in the form of aches in the stomach or head. It can be felt as a tightening of the jaws or clenching of teeth. Different people feel it in different ways. This is all totally natural. It is however, something that needs some comfort and calmness.

Stressing out about stressing out will just add to your stress. Instead of trying to get rid of the stress; try *adding* comfort and calmness. When you feel stress, see if you can pause and explore who or what can make the stress worse. This will help you find the most common patterns that signal your stress alarms, then instead of pushing it away, soothe it with a comforting breath and soft muscles.

That said, keep in mind that the triggers your emotional mind sees as dangerous aren't always immediately obvious. It may help to keep a stress journal over a week or two, to track the different triggers in your life and discover the ones that repeat themselves over and over and causes stress.

In your journal you can write down:

- What caused your stress (make a guess if you're unsure)
- How you felt, both physically and emotionally
- How you acted in response
- What you did to make yourself feel better (did you try to add comfort?)

We all respond to stress differently and there is no one-size-fits-all solution to fix stress overnight. Your own awareness and your quest for a better way will guide you to eventually reach a more peaceful state of mind.

Sincerely,

Libby

 Instead of taking away your stress, add some comfort.

Let's Get Some Comfort

Express your feelings instead of bottling them up. If something or someone is bothering you, talk about it in an open and respectful way.

Reframe problems. Try to view stressful situations from a more positive perspective. Rather than getting nervous because you have to wait in a long line, look at it as an opportunity to pause and breathe, observe your surroundings, or enjoy some alone time.

Look at the big picture. Think about the stressful situation and ask yourself how important it will be in the long run. Will it matter in a month? A year? Is it really worth getting upset over? If the answer is no, focus your time and energy elsewhere.

It's good enough to be good enough. Perfectionism is a major source of stress that can easily be avoided. Remember that we are all valuable, worthy and imperfect.

Let go of control. Many things in life are beyond our control—especially how other people act. Don't stress over them, rather take control of the choice you make to respond wisely.

Take care of yourself. Well-nourished bodies are better prepared to cope with stress, so make sure you eat balanced, nutritious meals throughout the day, try to stay away from too many sugary treats, and get enough sleep.

Comfort your stress instead of fighting it. Take a walk, connect with nature, call a friend, shake it out by jumping on a trampoline, take a long bath, listen to music, or engage in your favorite activity—and breathe.

I Hurt Myself

Dear Libby,

I have a problem. Whenever I get insulted or I feel hurt, I try to tell the person who made me feel that way how I feel. But my family never listens to me when I tell them anything. Sometimes I feel so sad when nobody listens that I go into my room, and I hurt myself in order to feel better. I don't know why that makes me feel better, but it does. Why am I doing that?

Hurting Inside and Out

Dear Hurting Inside and Out,

We all have to learn how to bear pain. It's not something we're born knowing how to do. Mostly, though, we either ignore the pain, or seek pleasure to cover up the pain. And sometimes, in our effort to push away the pain, we inadvertently end up creating another pain.

You ask why you're hurting yourself, your answer is hidden in the words you use to sign off. You hurt yourself, so that the outer pain overshadows the inner pain. It's hard to bear strong inner discomfort so your hurt yourself in a particular place, which narrows your attention to that area, moving the inner pain to the background. And that makes you feel better—for a short time—because the physical outside pain hurts a bit less than the pain you feel inside. Emotional pain is also physical pain. One is outside and one is inside. You have correctly defined it.

When we feel pain, we want to get rid of it very, very quickly. That's why we have lots and lots of painkillers. But when we try to kill pain, we don't learn how to manage pain. We humans have only two ways of dealing with pain. We either suppress it—by pretending it's not there, denying it, or pushing it away—or we bear it. Pretending doesn't really work. Bearing, while more difficult in the short term, helps us understand what it is, and enables us to do something about it. It's a very different process of dealing with pain—not by means of pleasure or pain to cover up the pain, but by integrating and blending pain with comfort. Instead of taking away pain, we add comfort.

So, when we feel physical pain of an emotional nature such as a tightness in the chest or an uneasiness in the stomach, we can place a warm bottle on the discomfort and then we breathe calmly. Sometimes just putting the palm of our hands on the chest will do. Simply inhaling and exhaling deeply can do a good job. Even just exhaling through the mouth can make a difference.

You can also try writing in a journal or going for a walk. If these things don't help, and if pain goes on for too long, hurts too deeply, and makes it hard for you to enjoy the good things in life, talking it out with someone who *will* listen can make it better.

Though it can be hard to build up the courage, sharing your feelings with someone you trust can help you sort through them. Saying out loud what's going on in your head, even if you think it doesn't make sense, helps clarify things that trouble you and adds comfort. It's a lot healthier, too. Carrying pent-up emotions creates a lot of physical tension in your body. When you get things off your chest, you can literally feel like a weight has been lifted.

Adults, especially trained professionals, have lots of experience dealing with many different problems, and won't usually get shocked by anything you tell them. Once you've decided to reach out for support, be honest, and you'll get honesty in return. Sometimes it's hard to ask for help because we think it makes us look weak or helpless. But the truth is—asking for help is a sign of strength.

Processing pain is not an overnight solution. It takes time. But the time and energy invested in doing so is transformative.

Adding comfort doesn't get rid of pain right away, but it means we learn better skills to listen to the pain. We come closer to it, connect to it, hear what it says, so that what is painful can have a voice that can tell us what's going on.

The ability to bear pain in a healthy way usually ensures that the pain doesn't come back so often. But if we just want to get rid of things quickly, we hurt and damage ourselves in the process. So, we eat a lot of sugar, or we cut ourselves. Some people use pain to cover up pain, some people use pleasure to cover up pain. In both cases we create a lot of self-harm. Everybody wants to run from pain in different ways, this is one. And while the immediate consequences of these different actions might be very different, essentially they are driven by the same impulse, to escape and kill pain, they are both compulsive and lack an ability to bear and tolerate pain and discomfort.

Try Using Breath as a Way to Manage Pain:

Start by breathing deeply, filling your belly like a balloon with breath-force while you inhale, then exhaling and releasing all hold of tension.

Breathe deeply in and out through every part of your body. Soften the muscles from the top of your head to the bottom of your feet, so that your jaw drops and your toes wiggle. Continue breathing; open every muscle, your body coming alive, your heart opening and relaxing, your throat softening, your face and eyes relaxing. Actively breathe in the openness of this moment.

This moment is alive. This moment exists. This moment is still, as still as the deep ocean. Feel the actual aliveness of this moment, living within you, living as you, and living all round you. Breathe.

Sincerely,

Libby

 When you hurt yourself outside, you create a purely physical pain that draws your attention away from an internal, emotional pain. Instead of using physical pain to draw your attention away from emotional pain, add comfort to manage the pain.

Final Thoughts

The Parable of the Trapeze

We move through life from stage to stage through periods of crises, discomfort and challenge.

In his book, *Warriors of the Heart*, Danaan Parry poetically describes life as a series of trapeze bar swings. At times we swing along comfortably on a familiar bar and at other times we find ourselves hurtling across space between bars. Of course, we can't get to the next bar without letting go of the old one. But hanging out in the space between trapeze bars can be a heart-stopping experience of uncertainty and suspense without any guarantee that we'll get to the other side. This discomfort can prevent us from letting go of the old to embrace the new.

> Mostly, I spend my time hanging on for dear life to the trapeze bar of the moment. . . . It carries me along a certain steady rate of swing and I have the feeling that I'm in control . . . But once in a while . . . I look ahead of me into the distance, and what do I see?
>
> I see another trapeze bar looking at me. It's empty. And I know, in that place in me that knows, that this new bar has my name on it. It is my next step, my growth, my aliveness coming to get me. In my heart of hearts I know that for me to grow, I must release my grip on the present well-known bar to move to the new one.
>
> Each time it happens, I hope—no, I pray—that I won't have to grab the new one. But in my knowing place, I know that I must totally release my grasp on my old bar, and for some moments in time I must hurtle across space before I can grab the new bar. Each time I do this I am filled with terror. It doesn't matter that in all my previous hurdles I have always made it.
>
> Each time I am afraid I will miss, that I will be crushed on unseen rocks in the bottomless basin between the bars.
>
> But I do it anyway. I must.

Transformation is not about making discomfort go away, but to allow ourselves to be there, between the bars, to hang in there and add comfort, so that change can happen.

"Yes," says Parry, "with all the fear that can accompany transitions, they are still the most vibrant, growth-filled, passionate moments in our lives."

~~~~~~~~~~

Make It Yours

Reflect on an area in your life where you are clinging to an outdated trapeze bar such as old patterns of behavior, unhelpful beliefs, or the sense of urgency to get rid of pain. How might you "let go" of that? Don't analyze this too much. Just write whatever wants to come out.

Holding on:

_____

Letting go:

_____

What is my one next step I can take that can bring me to my next bar?

_____

LISTEN

Chapter 4:

Listen to Yourself

Listen to the wind, it talks. Listen to the silence,
it speaks. Listen to your heart, it knows.

—NATIVE AMERICAN PROVERB

*W*ell-kept lawns and manicured gardens suggest that an area is being watched over by concerned and caring people. An abandoned lot, on the other hand, signals to passersby that it has been neglected by its owner. Anyone who's lived near empty property knows what that can look like. An overgrowth of weeds, broken-down fences, shards of glass, sundry trash and fallen branches indicate that there's no one tending this place.

In the previous chapters we discussed some ideas on how to cultivate our inner gardens. Like a well-kept lawn, we value it, care about it, keep an eye on it, and attend to it so that pretty blooms can blossom. In this chapter we explore how listening to yourself helps you tend to the garden that resides within you so that you can enrich and accentuate your friendships.

Listening to yourself helps you connect with who you are in the moment and find out about your needs and feelings so that you can take responsibility for them. *Response ability* is the ability to respond to your needs and feelings in an appropriate way. When you tune in to your inner self, the real and genuine you will let you know what's going on inside so that you can express it and do something about it. It also allows you to set and maintain proper boundaries, which are like invisible "fences" that protect you. Without boundaries, anyone can trespass: uninvited guests, unwelcome intruders, or other people's junk, because we're so empty and hungry that we allow anyone in or we've abandoned ourselves and don't care.

As we listen to ourselves, we find the voice that can carry us through life. The people in our environment can speak to us, and we can listen to what they say, but, eventually, we need to be guided from within. In listening, there's respect for everyone: yourself and others. What is true and good will resonate and emerge and connect us with one another in kindness. When we stop listening to our inner self, things become confusing and unclear. Separation, division, and conflict comes about only because we've forgotten or ignored the self.

When you know how to listen to yourself, you can let the outside world—people or situations—be what it may. You draw calmness and security from within, so you don't need to change or fix anyone. You're able to check in with your needs and pick up on your own yes and no, your okays, and not okays, and get guidance and direction from your internal GPS.

Your mind constantly oversees your needs, wishes, and dislikes, and communicates to you through the language of bodily sensations. If you take the time to slow down and tune in, you can listen to what it's saying: I'm hungry, I'm full, I'm hot, cold, thirsty, uncomfortable, in pain . . . Sometimes its messages are loud and clear: "Ouch! That hurts." Sometimes, they're quite subtle: a slight tightness in your chest, butterflies in your stomach, a heaviness, a lightness, or a feeling of expansion and openness.

The language of sensations helps you know what you need to know, just when you need to know it. For example, say you're walking down the street and you sense, even before you can think about it, a person who makes you feel uncomfortable moving toward you. Or, you answer the phone and before a word is spoken, you sense an uneasiness in your stomach, alerting you to an anger. How do you know this? It's your mind speaking to you through your body. You may even tell your friends about it, "I felt as though I'd been punched in the gut." Or, "I felt the shivers going down my spine."

That's your mind signaling to you via the language of body sensations, and it's worth paying attention to.

You can try this now. Start by imagining a peaceful and pleasurable situation and say "yes" to welcome it. Notice what your body is doing as you're welcoming it. Do you feel your chest open, does your stomach feel soft and relaxed, is your breath rhythmic and calm? Now think of a situation you would rather avoid and say the word "no" to reject it. Notice what happens. Do you feel your chest pulling in, does your head start shaking no, or do you feel uneasy and tight in your stomach? The sensations in your body act as a feedback system to inform you when a situation is a welcoming yes or a dismissive no.

Listening to ourselves is a skill that we can learn and practice. If you feel conflicted about a friendship that you have and you want to know if this friend is right for you or not, you can check inside with yourself and see if you get a yes or no response from your body. When you listen to yourself, you can start to notice that you resonate with some people and not others. You do things from a place of truth. You live with authenticity. You start to feel real and sincere and you tap into your personal strength. Take time to listen. Ask yourself, "What is this feeling telling me?" Then wait for an answer. It may not arrive right away, but with time and experience you can learn to trust it.

They Know How to Influence Me

Dear Libby,

I have a few friends who always manage to convince me to do things that I don't want to do, and then I find myself in hot water. I don't understand why this keeps happening.

*They know just how to influence me. I always
end up being a troublemaker and getting
punished. It's not fair. Please help me quickly.*

Needs Advice

Dear Needs Advice,

When others try to lead us and steer us in directions we are not sure
we want to take, it's hard to remain strong. Pressure from peers can
cause us to act or behave in ways that go against our values and better
judgement. Some people give in to peer pressure because they want
to be liked, they want to fit in, or because they're afraid that their
friends will laugh at them if they don't.

It takes a lot of courage to stand up and take personal responsibility
for your life and actually *own* your decisions. Whenever you're in
doubt, take a minute to tune in to your inner voice.

You have an inner voice that whispers to your heart. It says things
like, "I know this is right for me," or, "This doesn't feel good." These
whispers speak to you in interesting ways, often without using words
but rather signals that you can decipher. It's like a code language.
It's subtle, like a tingling sensation in your body or a gut feeling or a
tightness in the chest. Pay attention to how your mind speaks to you
through these physical sensations.

Most of us are accustomed to paying attention to signals from
outside ourselves—to what other people think and if they accept us
or not.

When we acknowledge that we have an inner voice that speaks to
us, it can take a bit of practice to listen and trust that voice. Once you
get the hang of it, you discover your own GPS to guide you. It's the
voice of truth that knows right from wrong. It speaks gently, but with

courage and with kindness. It is heard softly, but feels strong and clear, and it knows how to say "no."

The word *no* is important to set limits and boundaries, like invisible fences around your inner garden of truth. Our boundaries act like filters that let you sort through the information coming in from the outside and allow you to choose what you want to think and feel and do. These fences also protect you from stepping into other people's inner garden of truth, because you know that just like you, every person is responsible for their own thoughts, feelings, and actions.

So, when your friends try to convince you to do something, if that matches with your inner truth, you allow that to come through your filter. If it doesn't, you simply let that information bounce off your boundary. If you don't know if it's true or not, you look for more information about it, for example, by asking questions from parents or teachers.

Practice listening to your inner voice often. Challenge yourself. Before taking action, draw attention to the flow of air moving in and out of your nose. See if you can do it for thirty seconds, or for the count of ten. If you can manage for a minute or two, that's fabulous. This is the pause button that invites your body and mind to slow down and find out if this is something you want to do or not. As you observe your breath, notice the feelings or sensations in your body. A light, tingling sensation or a feeling of calmness and joy can be a positive response or a "yes." Feelings like heaviness, tightness in the chest, and tension in your body can be your inner voice saying "no."

It isn't always easy to be the one who says "no" to peer pressure, but you can do it.

It's a good idea to find a friend who shares similar values. Together you can support and strengthen each other to be influenced by your own inner voice rather than outer influences.

Sincerely,

Libby

Steve Jobs said, "Don't let the noise of others' opinions drown out your own inner voice."

Anger and Forgiveness

Dear Libby,

There was a girl who was mean to me a while ago. I know I should forgive her, but I don't want to. Also, I don't think it's fair that she was mean to me and gets to be forgiven. I don't want anything bad to happen to her, but I don't want to forgive her either. Please help me fast.

Bullied

Dear Bullied,

It seems that your question is about how to let go of anger when it feels unfair to do so. You feel like holding on to anger for the sake of justice, because if you let go of anger and forgive, then others get off scot-free. On the other hand, maybe something in you says you should forgive her since it doesn't feel nice to be angry.

Let's take a moment to understand what anger is. The body generates anger as a survival strategy to protect you in some way: like to stop people from hurting you, or to make sure that something upsetting doesn't happen again. Anger is like an alarm bell, warning you of danger, just like physical pain alerts you to pull your hand away from hot coals on a barbecue grill. It exists for a reason and deserves your attention and respect. It is a message that something isn't right. Although acting out anger (like attacking or hurting someone) is unhelpful at best and damaging at worst, anger in itself is a signal worth listening to.

So, why wouldn't you want to forgive this girl who was mean to you? Because you want to protect yourself. Clearly you think that even if you forgive her, she might do it again. Forgiveness is a way of letting somebody off the hook, and if someone did something hurtful, why should they be off the hook without restoring your sense of balance of justice and fairness? Is that okay? Did she apologize? Did she take responsibility for her actions? Did she say it wouldn't happen again?

At the same time, you say that you know you should forgive her. The question is, what is your motivation here? Why do you need to forgive her? So that others can approve of you? Because you need to be a nice person? When this girl was mean to you, and can repeat whatever she did, are you nice to yourself when you let that happen? Are you kind to yourself if you forgive?

You're asking a difficult question. If you forgive to relieve your guilt or avoid the disapproval of others, then you're not nice to yourself. You're angry. If you forgive and forget about your anger then you might be kind to others, but that kindness then excludes you. How can you be kind to yourself and others at the same time? Your dilemma is completely understandable.

Again, the fact that you're angry means an injustice has been done. You need to be kind to yourself in listening to that. As a matter of fact, it's only when you're kind to yourself that you find the way to forgive others. Only when your anger is a voice you listen to and understand and respect and learn from can you be kind to others and forgive them. Because anger doesn't want to hurt other people, it just wants to protect you. So, if you listen to your anger and learn to protect yourself, your anger will be satisfied, and you will act kindly to yourself and others, finding the space to forgive them as well.

That's essentially what anger is: a form of self-protection. And when we understand this, we can find other ways to protect ourselves. Then the anger can subside and we can forgive others. But we cannot forgive unless we feel safe.

You can feel safe by talking to this girl about what happened, and say, "Hey, that's not okay. How can we make sure that doesn't happen again?" If that feels too uncomfortable, perhaps you can ask somebody else to talk to her about it. Maybe you can distance yourself from her and ask for support from somebody, so you feel protected in the future. There are plenty of ways to make sure you'll be safe. Once you've listened to yourself, addressed the anger and worked through whatever was causing it, you will feel more relaxed and peaceful. When we feel calm understanding and forgiveness comes a lot more naturally. In turn, we feel lighter, freer, and open to connect again.

Sincerely,

Libby

 When we listen to the intense feelings in our body, we can respond with kindness.

Snobby, Nasty, and Bratty

Dear Libby,

There's a popular girl in my class who's very snobby. She's trying to fit into my group, but she's so nasty and bratty. My friends love her because they probably think they can become popular from her. She's really getting on my nerves. What should I do? I don't want her in my group.

Anonymous

Dear Anonymous,

How is it that a girl who's so popular and snobby wants to fit into your group? Don't you think that a girl who's so popular waits for everyone to fit into her group?

Maybe you're misunderstanding the meaning of her popularity.

Maybe she's trying so hard to make herself popular because she's afraid that otherwise nobody would be interested in her. She's so popular because she has a need to be accepted everywhere, and if she would be accepted everywhere she wouldn't be trying so hard to fit into your group, would she?

Behind snobbiness is somebody who is scared that if she isn't the star, she will be invisible. True, in their quest for popularity, they can be quite annoying as they go about making lots of noise that gives us a headache. We also meet a lot of people who play the game of snobbiness because they so desperately want us to believe that all is cool with them. How do we deal with that? How do we take responsibility for our feelings and needs? How do you say "no" and how do you say "yes"?

You might choose to say no. When you say no, you take less notice of her and just do your own thing. Nothing happens. Many people say no. Often, popular girls feel even more scared when we say no and they can react in different ways. You're not responsible for her experiences, but you can be kind about it. Even if you don't accommodate her, there's no need to be rude. In fact, setting boundaries means creating a space where kindness can happen.

Then again, you just might say yes.

You say yes, because you can see behind her outer facade and into the frightened heart beating under her chest. You know, in that place of knowing that she's actually trying so hard to be accepted and loved. And you just want to be kind.

If you do say yes to her, it has to be real and you must try to see it through. There's no yes/no. There's either a yes or a no. Both choices are okay. We don't have to expose ourselves to people who bring a lot of nastiness into our groups. We're allowed to say no, and it's good to learn how to say no with kindness. Kindness always leads the way. We needn't be judgmental or harsh. We just have to decide whether it's a yes or a no.

Sincerely,

Libby

 When you look beyond popularity and snobbiness you can make real choices about saying yes or no. ♡

Tell Me What's Wrong

Dear Libby,

I have a lot of friends, and we spend a lot of time together. My problem is when I see that my friends are sad I care so much that I want them to tell me what's wrong. They don't always want to talk about it, and I get upset. Sometimes I feel like they don't trust

*me, but I know that's not true. Also, I have
a really close friend, who I really love, but
sometimes I get very annoyed with the way
she speaks. She's very blunt. Can you please
tell me how to deal with these issues which
come up very often?*

Frustrated, age 16

Dear Frustrated,

Your ability to tune in to what's going on inside you and around you will tell you when your relationships are connecting and when they're not. While it's natural to wish for a relationship that lingers forever, it often means that we don't have a strong enough connection with ourselves and that we don't want to feel alone.

Friendships need to have that space where sometimes we're available and sometime we're not, sometime we're blunt and sometimes we're soft. Sometimes friends share and sometimes they don't, because things may be going on for them which they're not able or ready to share. And we need to be able to weather the different degrees of connection that exist within a friendship.

So, when there's a disconnect for a time, how can we bear it? When we note what's going on and listen to our feelings of uneasiness, we don't need to follow the instructions the discomfort gives us. You see, uneasiness is uncomfortable, and our immediate impulse is to want to put an end to that feeling fast—in the blink of an eye, if only we could. But that doesn't really work. Instead, trying to get rid of discomfort just adds more discomfort.

Listening to the uneasiness without acting on it will let us know what we need right now. In your situation, when your friend doesn't want to share, it may just not be the right time to share. And when somebody is blunt, they may not be available for a relationship right now. Listening to yourself isn't about making the blunt person less blunt or making someone share right now. It means listening to your need, pausing, and finding wisdom in how you can meet that need without forcing anybody to give you connection.

Possibly, the solution lies in finding connections elsewhere, with other people for a time. It could also be that we supply part of it on our own—and reconnect with ourselves.

There are many ways this can be done. A good way to start is by sensing the air going in and out of your nose. I know, this sounds very simplistic. Nevertheless, don't forget that breathing is what keeps us alive, and by sensing the flow of our breath moving in and out of our nose, we might even sense—in a very tangible way—that we're alive. That's a nice thing to sense! And, if the breathing is calm and gentle and satisfying, it can feel very nurturing, almost like we're giving ourselves a hug.

So we can listen to ourselves and know what our need is (in this case, the need is connection). Without ignoring what the uneasiness is telling you to do (make someone say something or fix someone), you can pause and gently resist following its instructions. Instead, breathe, bear the discomfort and supply the connection you need by reconnecting with yourself until you find a comfortable, wise way to respond to the need.

Sincerely,

Libby

 Listen, pause, and learn to endure discomfort until you find a wise response.

Too Shy to Speak Up

Dear Libby,

My friends are mean to me, and I can't stand it. I'm too shy to say anything to them. So, what should I do?

Bullied by Friends, age 13

Dear Bullied,

No one likes or deserves to be mistreated. To be able to say something to someone, we need to check in with ourselves and listen to what our feelings are telling us. The more specific you can be about what your friends are doing, the more you'll be able to speak up about what's bothering you. Do they hit you? Do they bump into you? Do they say unkind words to you? Get down to the details. Sometimes we're shy because we're not sure what to say.

See if you think about it in terms of *movements*. That will give you more clarity, and then you'll know what to say. Raising a hand is a movement, making a face that expresses dislike or disrespect is a movement. Once you identify what the movement is, you can express what's happening, share how you feel about it and make a request for change. For example, "When you . . . (fill in the movement: make a face, speak angrily, or grab something from me), I feel . . . (fill in how the movement makes you feel: sad, hurt, uncomfortable, or angry?) Please stop."

Sincerely,

Libby

When you define the situation you can express the situation.

The Influence Effect

Dear Libby,

My class acts very, very, very immature. They're influencing me, and, before I know it, I get sent out of class. It just hit me that they're influencing me!

Influenced

Dear Influenced,

Wow, it sounds like you've learned about the power of influence. Other people, our environment, even the weather can influence our behavior, our feelings, and our thoughts. Now that you've learned about the effects of negative influence, it's time to learn about the effects of positive influence. You can do it! Inside of you, there's a whisper, a small voice only you can hear. Don't count on others to be responsible for you. Listen to your own inner voice, and you'll be a shining example of mature behavior, which will influence everyone around you.

Sincerely,

Libby

Become a person of influence to positively
impact the lives of others.

Part-Time Friend

Dear Libby,

*I have a friend who lives in my
neighborhood and is in my class. At school, we
argue a lot and don't talk to each other. But
at home, we get along like best friends. I'm
really confused.*

Confused

Dear Confused,

A *part-time* friend, unlike a part-time job, can make you feel very
confused. Mixed messages make us feel mixed-up. When we see two
road signs which contradict, we don't know how to move forward,
and we feel bewildered.

This can happen when a friend is sending opposite signals. It can
also happen when we are in conflict between what we know inside to
be true and what we want to be true. Sometimes the truth makes us
feel uncomfortable, and we'd rather linger in that no-man's land we
call confusion then feel the pain.

When you sense something strange is going on, it usually is.
Sometimes a friendship can go through a rough patch in order to

improve, but if you keep feeling funny about a situation, and it keeps coming up again and again, it does need to be attended to.

Either you have a best friend or you don't.

A "friend" who is only there for you when it's convenient, only available when there's something she needs from you, is not a best friend. Friendship is built on consistency and trust.

You might want to have a conversation with your friend. Share how you're feeling. If you enjoy spending time with her, tell her so. If you're wondering about what's going on, ask her about it. If you find that she's not open to discuss anything or that the conversation turns into another fight, then it may help you see the truth that you were trying to ignore.

But then you will know this person is not a real friend, and you will no longer be confused. You will be able to let go, because you know that you can't control another person or force a friendship. Letting go means that you don't try to blame another person but try to make the most of yourself. If your friend expresses surprise and chooses to reconnect, that's great. Just be careful about how much hope you allow. As hard as it may feel right now, sometimes when friends go their separate ways, it's actually a blessing in disguise.

In the meantime, don't fight your feelings—rather, try to find something inside yourself that's bigger than those feelings. There's lots of strength within you, and now's the time to find it.

Here are some tips that may help ease the process:

1. Write a letter to your friend that you never intend to send. This is a safe way for you to share how the ending of this friendship affected you. It gives you the chance to say things that haven't been said, and to say goodbye. After you put your feelings on paper and you understand yourself better, you may want to discard it so that you can start a "new page" in your life.
2. Gently encourage yourself to take part in activities that bring new people into your life. Write a list of your hobbies, family

members, supportive teachers, kind neighbors, etc. Then write a list of at least five inner strengths, like a sense of humor, imagination, determination, etc. Just writing the list can help you find your inner strength and feel more open to the goodness in the world. Do this every day. The more you can add to your list, the more you'll realize the world is an endless source of resources.

3. Keep things neutral. It may seem obvious, but don't try to get your other classmates to take sides. Get comfortable with the fact that they may still spend a great deal of time with your lost friend and this is not a reflection on you. Resist bad-mouthing her to others. It will only make you look bad. If you need to vent, reach out to someone who's totally outside of the situation.

Ending a friendship isn't easy, but, often, it leads your life in a new, better direction. By letting go, you free up more time to for healthier, more satisfying friendships, and you'll likely learn a little more about yourself in the process.

That said, look for opportunities where you can meet more girls. Join a new club. Sit down next to someone you'd like to get to know better. Invite her to partner with you on a project you enjoy doing. Only when we're brave enough to listen to our truth and face it, are we able to move from confusion to clarity.

Sincerely,

Libby

 Confusion sometimes happens when we try to hold on to what we want to believe while dismissing our intuitive signals.

My Friend Gets Bullied

Dear Libby,

Although I love school, there's a serious bullying issue in my class. I'm friends with a girl in my class that nobody likes. There is a specific girl who really dislikes her. She picks on her terribly. Thank goodness, I'm not being bullied, but it really hurts me to see my friend being bullied while nobody is doing anything about it. I've discussed this with my parents, but they don't have an answer. Is it worth it to be friends with this girl and risk being picked on? I've tried including a teacher, but even that doesn't help. What should I do?

Feels Threatened

Dear Feels Threatened,

Unlike the bully or the one being bullied, you, as a bystander, can make the choice of either being part of the problem (hurtful bystander) or part of the solution (helpful upstander). Ignoring bullying or walking away in relief that "at least it's not me," is the easy way out. When we turn a blind eye and pretend we don't see, we give bullies our silent okay to carry on doing what they're doing—it sends a message to the bully that this behavior is acceptable.

It's great that you've tried including your teacher. It takes courage to stand up for human rights—and you did. Good for you. But if it didn't help, you needn't give up. Bullying is unacceptable, and anyone who witnesses it should do whatever they can to put a stop to it. Every single child, and adult, is entitled to live with dignity and without fear and pain.

At the same time, we need to act with care and wisdom. If you were walking by a lake and saw someone drowning, what is the best action to take? Should you dive in? Call for help? Throw her a line? These are questions we should ask ourselves and seek answers for.

There's a classic formula of rescue that lifeguards learn. When they see someone drowning, the first thing they do is call for help. Then, they reach, throw, and, lastly, go. If the victim is close enough, they reach out to offer a hand. If the victim is too far out, they throw the safety ring or row out. If all else fails, they jump in to rescue the victim. We can see that extending an anchoring arm for the victim to lift herself out of the water is the optimal choice. Jumping into the lake is the option of last resort, because it endangers both parties.

Maybe we can apply the same principles to helping a victim of bullying. First, you call for help, as you've done, by including your teacher. Don't give up. If she doesn't help, maybe you can speak to the principal about it. Next, just like a swim safety class would teach, you reach, throw, and go. Reach out to her with kindness and encouraging words. Throw her a rope: offer her the support that she needs to find the strength to "pull back to shore" and stand up for herself. Connect with an open heart, tune into her experience as if it was your own. Ask yourself what you would be feeling if you were her, and how you would've wanted to be supported. And finally, go. Encourage her to ask for help from an adult. Offer to go along as a support.

You can spread kindness instead of the gossiping and teasing that's happening, and by all means, avoid laughing along with the bully, make it clear that you won't be involved in any of this. Don't just be a bystander, be an *upstander*.

Sincerely,

Libby

 Putting a stop to bullying is up to you. It's up to all of us.

She Clings to Me

Dear Libby,

There's a girl in my class who I'm friends with, but not best friends. She thinks I'm her best friend and wants to go shopping and out to eat. I have fun with her, and I don't mind walking home with her sometimes, but I don't want her to cling to me. I know it's about kindness and everything, and I want to be nice to her, but I don't like the relationship we have now. She talks negatively about my other friends and sometimes says inappropriate things. I don't know how to tell her, and I don't want to hurt her feelings. Please help!

Doesn't Want a Clinger

Dear Doesn't Want a Clinger,

For many people, it's difficult to set boundaries or say no to others. When we say yes to everything out of fear of other people's reactions, we don't respect our personal limits. We end up feeling stressed, overwhelmed and resentful. Setting boundaries with people can help you create better friendships in the long run. The friends you want to choose are those who, even if they initially feel upset or disappointed, will respect your limits.

A lack of boundaries is like a garden without a fence—anyone can come in at any time and treat your space like it's their space. Limits and boundaries are a way to take care of and respect your time, your energy, and your personal space. It sends a clear message that there's no trespassing here. You are not an extension of other people; you are your own, separate self.

Without this invisible fence, it's easy to get caught up in other people's storms or hurricanes—bad moods, pity parties, or words and actions that affect or wound you.

When we say no to things that distress us, we're saying yes to sincerity and genuine caring. Remember that boundaries create a space that allows for kindness to happen. Kindness is inclusive, and you as a person also get to be included in your kindness.

In the same way that fences add beauty to a garden, boundaries in friendships accentuate and enrich friendships. They ensure that your interactions are healthier, and that you can truly enjoy your time together.

Knowing how to set boundaries takes skill and time. It is a process. Listen to yourself, determine what is going on inside and then express yourself kindly, respectfully, and assertively: "This kind of talk isn't appropriate for me. I don't speak badly about my friends." Or, "Thanks for the invitation to go shopping, but I'd rather not." There's nothing hurtful about setting proper boundaries.

Sincerely,

Libby

Boundaries create a space that allows for kindness to happen. ♡

~~~~~~

Hurtful Words

Dear Libby,

I have diabetes. Girls in my class make fun of me in front of everyone. I get very embarrassed. They call me Diabetes Girl. If I ask if I can play they say, "No, because we don't play with girls with diabetes." I try to ignore them, but it does not help. Please help me fast.

Girl with Diabetes

Dear Girl with Diabetes,

It is painful to be called names for a condition which you didn't choose. Teasing, hurtful, and unkind words that are intentional and constant is called bullying. I encourage you to do everything in your power to put a stop to this. Living with diabetes may be challenging, but it doesn't take away from your special value as a very precious person.

Ask your parents to talk to your teacher, your principal, and/or the parents of the girls who bully you—whoever they feel will help nip this in the bud.

In addition, try using what I call the **VIP** method for **VIP** kids:

- V: Visualize yourself wearing an emotional raincoat. Any time someone say hurtful word, they just slide off like raindrops without getting absorbed inside.
- I: I-messages can help you express your feelings without inviting more teasing by speaking calmly and assertively. Here's an example, "I feel upset when you call me names. I would like you to stop."
- P: Play it Cool. While your hurt feelings may be there, see if you can pay attention to your breath, and soften your muscles in your face and chest. This will help you stay present and add calmness and confidence to your body. It also sends a nonverbal message to the bully about your inner strength.

The VIP method takes the fun out of the bully's attempts to get to you. When bullies fail to get a response from you, they often lose interest. But more importantly, when you have a gentle, rhythmic, and nourishing breath, you'll be able to access the wise part in you that knows how to best protect yourself.

Sincerely,

Libby

 Visualizing, using I-messages and playing it cool will help you stay present in the face of a bully.

Using I-Messages:

Sometimes things happen between friends that activate powerful movement energy, which is the fight-or-flight response to something the mind perceives as threatening. As a result, we either attack, scream, blame (fight) or withdraw, clench our jaws or pretend as though all's cool (flight). Neither way is the optimal response, of course. They both lead to misunderstandings, confusion and a lot of hurt.

It's hard to put big feelings into words, or to organize our thoughts and speak with strength and kindness in those intense moments. This is where I-messages can be very helpful. It's a short and sweet formula that helps you listen to your thoughts and feelings and express your truth with love and respect.

Here is an example of the difference between a "you" message and an "I" message:

"You" message: "You're so nasty. You're always hurting me and saying mean things to me."

"I" message: "I heard you say that I'm weird. I feel pain about that. I need to feel accepted for who I am. I want to ask you to speak kindly."

An "I" message can have four parts:

1. **You share what happened:** Identify the concrete, technical movement that was made. Words were spoken, hands went up, etc. This helps you stay focused and accurate. Saying, "I heard you tell me to leave the game

because I have diabetes," is describing a specific fact, not a story that can be interpreted in different ways.

2. **You share how you feel:** Feelings connect us on a heart-to-heart level. "I feel sad."

3. **You share what you need:** When we express our needs, we have a better chance of getting them met. "I need to feel included in the group regardless of my condition, which I didn't choose."

4. **You share what you want to happen:** Sharing what we want, instead of what we don't want, gives others a clear and positive direction. "I would like to be able to join the games just like everyone else."

Help Me, Fast

Dear Libby,

Almost two years ago, I made a very sweet friend. She is a very quiet girl while I'm a very loud girl. She talks so, so quietly, and she never plays sports. But on the other hand, she's a very good friend. We shared each other's secrets and successes. We studied together and spoke together. But something happened this year that changed it all. I made friends with a girl I'll call Sara, and she became our third friend. But Sara opened my eyes to the world, and I realized

*that she's much more my type. She is as
loud as I am, and goes swimming with me
(my first friend was scared). The problem is
that our friendship doesn't really work as a
trio, and we end up in fights. But to tell you
the truth I want Sara rather than my old
friend. However, I don't want to drop my
old friend. Please help me fast.*

Waiting for Help

Dear Waiting for Help,

Relationships and how they evolve and develop is not something that happens fast. It's something that requires sensitivity and wisdom. Getting "fast" help is not helpful. The greater the sense of urgency and the faster you want to find a way out of a conflict, the less effective your solution will be. Fast thinking is dedicated for dangerous situations in which you need very quick answers, like how to find the nearest exit when there's a fire in the room.

In situations where your physical survival is not at stake, slow, deliberate thought can help you figure out a mathematical formula, write a thought-provoking essay, and remember information on a test. Slow, deliberate thinking also helps you navigate life situations like matters of friendship with better results.

Swift answers lead to quick fixes and half-baked solutions that don't last long or address only part of the issue. So, perhaps hastily, you decide: "Let's be a trio." When that doesn't work you come up with a new speedy solution: "Replace your old friend." Well that doesn't work because you don't want to lose your old friend. Quick strategies to escape discomfort don't provide complete solutions. They are reactive, impulsive, and often based on worry and fear.

Sometimes it's the long lane that brings you to your destination sooner. Taking fast action can lack balance and harmony. It can lead to more complications along the way. On the other hand, slowing down and gently resisting impulsivity allows you to create a space for your wise inner guide to direct you. Wisdom sees a broader picture. It takes more things into consideration, and weaves together several threads for richer, more effective solutions.

If you're prepared to pause and not act until you know *how* to act, you will suddenly experience a sense that something just feels like the right thing to do. That still, small voice within you knows. For example, it may ask, "Is there a way to hold on to both friendships while liking them differently?"

Then, instead of rushing around for a fast answer, you make yourself comfortable with the question. Learn about the question. Savor the question. And then wait for something inside of you to give you an answer. A wise solution will naturally arise.

For example, you might suddenly see three types of trees in the garden and notice how they all look differently and yet they each add something to the other. The way the three trees look better than just two trees growing side by side may offer a new understanding of your dilemma. It can inspire you with its beauty and give you a sense that you know how to manage a friendship made of three. As you hang out with the question, something you see, hear, or read will lead to a flash of insight and provide an answer.

Sometimes, you will feel curious to reach out and ask others to share their ideas and wisdom. Learning from people's experiences is another way to gain wisdom.

If you don't seek an instant solution, if you can be patient with the question and let it be there even as you go on with your life, answers show up in the most interesting places. You just know it when you see it: "That's an idea for me! That's just what I need to do."

Sincerely,

Libby

Fast solutions are quite limited in scope, whereas patience and stillness make room for wiser and intuitive knowing.

My Friend Snobs Me Out

Dear Libby,

I have a friend who's very close to me . . . I think . . . But she's also friends with another girl who acts as if it's below her to look at me. Whenever I appear when they're together, my friend snobs me out. What should I do?

Best Friends (Maybe), age 13

Dear Best Friends,

Experiences like these indicate that there is room for self-reflection. It may be time to assess whether the relationships we are in are good for us or not and if we're handling our part of it in the right way. This is an opportunity for you to practice listening to yourself.

Ask yourself the following questions:

1. How do I feel when I spend time with my friend? Do I feel safe and comfortable to be myself and to reveal my fears and vulner-abilities, or do I feel compelled to act and conform in a way that pleases and impresses my friend?
2. Can I grow with this friend at my side, or does my growth feel stifled from negative talk and behavior?

3. Does my friend build my sense of self or does she belittle me with hurtful comments?

4. Is it a mutual friendship? Do we respect each other, do we feel for each other, do we act with kindness to each other?

While we want to be kind and respectful to every person, we choose the friends we'd like to connect with to build an authentic and meaningful friendship.

Sincerely,

Libby

 Taking time to reflect on our friendships matters.

I Need Some Air

Dear Libby,

I have a friend who is always around me. She is very nice, but I need some air. I don't want to tell her, because she'll get insulted. Please help me.

Out of Air

Dear Out of Air,

Your friend doesn't mean to be stifling; she's just not aware of how she might be disturbing you.

Friendship is about mutual respect and admiration that creates a special space for two people to become more of who each of them are. When you're being nice to someone instead of being real, you're not being true to who you are. Hiding behind a mask of being nice when inwardly you feel like screaming is not true kindness. Try to set boundaries within your friendship. Every person is entitled to their personal space. For instance, you can say, "I enjoy spending time with you because you are a very nice person. Please understand when I take time for myself, it doesn't mean that I don't like you anymore. I just need a little me time."

Sincerely,

Libby

 Kindness without truth is like a mask without a person. It's pretend play, not friendship.

Love Your Neighbor, But It's Hard

Dear Libby,

We know it's important to love your fellow neighbor, however sometimes it's very hard. We're two friends, and there's another girl who wants to stick to us. She's not our cup of tea but dropping her may cause a broken heart. We need help ASAP!

Troubled

Dear Troubled,

If your understanding is that loving your fellow neighbor is the truth, then the fact that it is hard, just means it's hard. And you do it anyway. More than that, you might need to ask yourself why it's so hard. What is so hard about being kind? Furthermore, if somebody sticks to you and puts forth unreasonable expectations, then does being kind to that person allow you also to be kind to yourself? If it does, then the fact that it is hard just means that you have an opportunity to grow into becoming a kinder person and learning that to be kind is something that you can enjoy. But if you find that her demands are beyond kindness to yourself then your growth may come from learning how to say no.

It happens in friendships, when two people create a very nice situation where there's love and kindness and goodwill, that another person will come along and say, "Can you please adopt me? Can I be the little girl in this 'family'?" Of course, you can be kind and considerate, but you can't pretend that it's a friendship, because it's not. Kindness is how we share the message, with tact and respect and empathy.

That said, when we call a friendship a cup of tea then it's probably worth wondering what kind of tea it is and why do we drink it? Are you drinking tea because it makes you feel special? This is not a question that needs to be answered right now, but it is a question that can lead to other questions. Sometimes we need to consider whether we're part of a tea club to separate from others or whether its purpose is to connect with friends in an authentic way.

Many people like to belong to an exclusive tea club. It makes them feel unique and special but apart from drinking tea, they don't really do much else. Sometimes, though, we forge a bond between a group of friends to express ourselves, to grow and develop ourselves, to give and receive and share joy. When other people come along who don't share our values, who cause dissent and friction, we may need to kindly and gently decline their request to join.

But when we have the feeling that somebody is not our cup of tea, we would be wise to question why we are saying that. Are we allowing the power of the group to cover up our lack of kindness? Or, is this a real genuine question about how to tell somebody—in the kindest way possible—that we don't want to play with them. There might be room for some self-reflection here.

Sincerely,

Libby

 Kindness may not always be easy, or always feel good, but what sort of person do you want to be?

Final Thoughts

Living from the inside can reset and upgrade your experience in life. Tune in to honest, wise, simple you, and encourage your questions or answers to come without thinking or analyzing. Simply allow the words to emerge.

Create a safe space where you can write directly from your innermost self. Let the stream of words surface without censorship, without rereading them, but simply as a spontaneous flow for juicy, fresh, direct, quirky, but right on target thoughts and ideas.

Make It Yours

Keep a notebook handy and enjoy companionable time with it. Have fun writing, doodling, sketching, or jotting down daily observations—the poetry of your heart. Play with broad, bold strokes, using pens of different colors for different days, ideas, or moods. Feel free to be messy, make mistakes and express yourself in any way you like.

EXPRESS

Chapter 5:

Express Yourself

Our deepest fear is not that we are inadequate.
Our deepest fear is that we are powerful beyond
measure. It is our light, not our darkness,
that most frightens us . . . And as we let our
own lights shine, we unconsciously give
other people permission to do the same.

—MARIANNE WILLIAMSON

*W*hen you express yourself, you share with the world the natural radiance of who you are: your thoughts, feelings, ideas, and experiences, the unique imprint of your individuality. Everything about you—the way you speak, the way you listen, the way you draw or doodle or sing or walk—is artistic and conveys a rare felicity and grace of expression: yours. There never was and there will never be anyone quite like you.

When you aspire to express the life in you, life collaborates to express itself through you. It becomes a mutual expression, life and you, creating and expanding together. Time seems to stand still, hours merge and intermingle in beautiful hues as you color the glass of life's mosaic assigned only to you. You are loving life and feel fully alive, present in the moment, experiencing the joy of being. What makes creative self-expression so enchanting is that you find in the art you offer the world, the reflection of your innermost self.

Nobody has ownership over talent and capabilities. There are no talent stores where you must come and purchase a cup of talent. Talents are available to everyone, like the air around us. You can connect to any new skill or talent that you are drawn to. You then become a conduit, allowing talent to come through you to add joy to the world. Merely by pursuing what you find fascinating and engaging in the activities that bring you life, you will express who you are and develop your talents. If you love to dance, go dance. If you like the cello then play it. If you like cleaning walls with reverse graffiti, then do that. In the process of doing what you enjoy, you will learn how.

You have something profound within you that wants to be shared with the world. You have the capacity to make a real difference, to inspire another person, to touch someone's life. Listen to the whispers of your heart, and let them guide you, number by number, piece by piece, color by color, and you will be amazed by what you can create. Creativity doesn't require membership or contracts where you must sign on the dotted line. Creativity is yours—your birthright as a human being.

After the lights dim and the curtains close, and the show is over, and you've tasted enough drama, creative self-expression happens when you discover that doing things for the sole purpose of being loved, visible, and approved of by others has become . . . well, boring. You begin to brush your strokes on the canvas and paint your masterpiece, or draw, or bake, or climb mountains, simply because you find that doing so animates and exhilarates *you*. You engage in art or music or poetry not because of a wish to be noticed and acknowledged by other people but because of the pleasure it brings you. You experience your talents as life's gifts to you, not as your entry pass to belonging or acceptance.

If you love to paint, you allow the picture to emerge from you onto the canvas. If you love to make people laugh, you enjoy the humor that springs forth from you. If baking petit fours and triple layer tiramisu cakes makes you come alive, you allow it to come forth through you.

Express yourself and find your will and your voice. You will get to entertain yourself for your own sake (not to be popular, accepted or adored). You will discover your personal destiny, your calling, your purpose. You will become who you always were but were afraid to embrace. You will learn that your talents are not your bid for attention, but a gift to the world and every being in it.

Inspiration will put ideas into your lap as a reward for your enthusiasm and your devotion. You will acquire humility because you know that you are not the source of the creations—you just allow its coming into being through you.

~~~~~~~~~~~~~~~~~~~~~~~~~~~~~~~~~~~~~~

Getting in the Way of My Happiness

Dear Libby,

I hate myself for having this problem because I created it. I have an amazing life. I'm not deprived of anything. I get in the way of my own happiness and that makes me so mad. My problem is that I don't really have friends. And by really I mean that I know a lot of nice girls who I like and who like me. I've known them all for a while and technically we're close. The problem is that I never hang out with anyone, like a normal teenager. I don't even know why. I just always stay at home. I haven't let myself create memories for some reason. I get all anxious thinking about sleeping over at someone's, going to their house, etc. And I'm always beating myself up over this, because I'm not letting

*myself live! I don't even know when it started,
I just know I want it to end. I know it's up
to me, but, for some reason, I just can't push
myself to do anything about it. Please help.*

Needs Help

Dear Needs Help,

It seems you're so preoccupied with escaping pain that you have forgotten to live, as you write, "I'm not letting myself live." What happens is that when we're afraid of pain and try to run from it, we get into loops of thoughts about pain, and we end up feeling pursued by it. And then life passes us by. The one thing that you're not prepared to accept is that there will be pain. Stop running from it. If you're not prepared to have pain, then you can't live.

Let me show you what I mean. Imagine you're in your house looking at the playground through the window and wondering how much it will hurt when you fall off the swing. And you will fall off the swing, because everybody falls off the swing. But you need to decide whether or not you are prepared to enjoy the delights of swinging as well as the disappointments of falling.

All we can do in life is make sure that we enjoy the fun of the park more often than the inevitable tumble. If all we do is hang back in fear of the failures and frustrations of life, we don't live, because life has already stopped. Instead of swinging with the ups and downs we're on a continuous chain of falling off the swing before we've even reached out to touch it.

You realize that. You just don't understand that this is what is happening to you.

What's happening is simply your wish to escape from pain or discomfort. We need to embrace pain—not wish it upon ourselves, but know that it's part of life, and we need to be prepared to live anyway. Joy and sorrow are two parts of the same coin of life. We can't have one without the other. Once you're prepared to have pain by saying to yourself, *I will have pain. And it will be okay. I'll find a way to cope with that. And now let's open the door and get on that swing.*

You may begin to wonder, "Which parts of the 'playground' attract me the most?" not, "Which ones am I the most scared of?"

Maybe you want to share what you have with others. Maybe you want to express yourself in ways that will make your friendships special, not just technical.

Any kind of *movement toward* something you find exciting is an act of self-expression. Right now, you are *moving away*, withdrawing and retreating to yourself, because you don't want to have pain. If instead, you move toward life, prepared to face what comes your way—both the comforts and the discomforts—you will be able to experience the happiness you know is there, and let yourself live.

Every time that "swing" in your mind, says, "It's gonna hurt." tell it, "Yes it will. But it will also be fun." Eventually there'll be more fun than hurt. Chances are you won't just see the shadowy parts on the playground of life, you'll see the sunshine too.

Sincerely,

Libby

 Don't just stare at the swing of life afraid that you may tumble; get on it and have a good time.

~~~~~~

Are They Talking about Me?

Dear Libby,

I have a complex that anytime I see people talking, I always think that they are talking about me. How can I get rid of this complex?

Ashamed

Dear Ashamed,

Instead of trying to get rid of this perception that people are talking about you, why don't you add more of yourself talking about you? We tend to get so busy figuring out what people are saying, or not saying, or how they are saying it, that we forget to hear what we ourselves are saying. Turn on the volume of your own voice, and the voices of others will become less important.

Let people say what they have to say. Even better, let them enjoy what they have to say. If they have something to express, that's great, so do you. Instead of focusing on what people are saying, simply start bringing to life what you have to say. The way you express yourself may look different from the way they do. It may come through art, dance, music, or anything you like. When you get busy enjoying your own self-expression, with energy, focus, and dedication, you won't give a dime for the opinions of others.

Is there anything you would like to talk about, or express? To find out, ask yourself: What excites me? What do I enjoy doing? Your life is an adventure to find your mission and your calling. Let your inquisitive mind lead you in your search. Trust it. Let it be your torch light escorting you through secret doors and hidden alleys and underground routes until you discover your passion.

Go to museums and find out what sparks your interest. Visit the library and browse the titles to see what resonates with you. Go to the beach and watch the sea and clear space in your mind where ideas will find room to emerge and grow. Have a journal or index cards to jot down some notes and allow yourself to dream of a new world. Keep your eyes open. Follow your curiosity. Continue to ask questions.

- What do you love doing for others?
- What do you find fascinating, inspiring and uplifting?
- What have others always told you you're good at?
- If all you had left was today what would you do?
- What would you add if you were granted an extra 1 month, 6 months, 1 year, and 5 years?

Consider asking people close to you—often others can see things about us that we don't. Take time to discuss your ideas with adults in your life whom you hold in the highest regard. Or, visit a senior citizen home and ask them about their lives. Questions may lead to more questions. See what information comes your way.

- What do your parents, siblings, or friends like to share about you?
- What do they think you might enjoy doing?
- How did they choose to do what they're doing?
- How did they get good at it?
- How are they making a difference in the world, and how can you be inspired by them?

Questions and answers can be a springboard to explore your unique self. Take joy in your growth. The last thing you need is to get distracted by people huddling together and talking, whether about you or anyone else. Find the security inside of you as you explore the incredible and spellbinding things you can discover and say about yourself.

Sincerely,

Libby

 Just because some people have a view about things in life, you needn't let it stop you from giving expression to your own life.

~~~~~~~~~~~~~~~~~~~~~~~~~~~~~~~~

Does She Like Me?

Dear Libby,

I have a friend I like a lot, and who I think about a lot, even when we're not together. The thing is, I don't know if she feels the same way about me. What can I do to figure out this relationship that's so important to me?

Friendly

Dear Friendly,

When two friends enjoy spending time with each other, and they want to figure out how they feel about each other, they just ask. It's not difficult to ask, but we often shy away from doing so, because we don't want to be hurt. We're scared that we might not like the answer we get.

When another person becomes more important to me than I am to me, then I have stopped living my own life. You see, all living things grow and develop and expand and express themselves, like a garden in continuous bloom.

Your life, too, with its constant unfurling beauty, has infinite depth, and potential. The treasures inside you are boundless and measureless, unceasingly forming you into the best you. But, if you allow yourself to be overshadowed by a friend who you've turned into a sun, you interrupt the spontaneous expression of yourself. You no longer see that you shine, because you've forgotten that you're a sun yourself, not just a moon.

There's only one you. Nobody can shine their light quite like you. Some people think they must earn their right to reveal their light. You don't. Believe in your own identity and in that which is alive in you that makes you unique. Who you are can express itself if you let it. Creative self-expression is organic to you, it is the way you walk and the way you talk, it is your signature and style, as much a part of you as the color of your eyes or the timbre of your voice.

Once you know that you shine brightly, you will no longer feel the need to rely on someone else's light. When you can sense and trust your own brightness, your question about whether or not your friend feels the same as you, will not be so important to you. Don't be surprised when you discover that!

In the meantime, when you're not together with your friend, see if you can redirect your attention from thoughts about her, to thoughts about you. This means that you sense your own body in the room, before you sense hers. In your mind, that is. Because every time you think about your friend, your deeper mind senses her presence, and that's your opportunity to practice sensing your own presence first. When you can have a strong sense of yourself in the room, taking up space, a living being breathing softly, you can access the treasure house within you. You have everything you need to live life joyously and creatively.

Many people are cut off from the sweetness and satisfaction which lies *within* themselves, because they crave it from the world *outside* themselves: from people, from chocolate, or from amusement parks. Sensing your physical self and the flow of air moving in and out of your nose, will lift you out of confusion, insecurity, and lack. It will guide you to your own vitality, peace of mind, and creative self-expression.

Make your room bright. Hang up posters, create some interesting decor for your bedroom, whatever suits your fancy. When the room is yours, and you are there, and you discover that you're like a sun, not a moon, you can invite your friend to join you, either in real life, or even in your imagination for some practice. Know that you have lots of light to offer to others.

Sincerely,

Libby

 If life came with a disclaimer on a tag, it would say something like this: This is yours. Use it well. Don't give it away. It is to be expressed through you.

Love to Laugh

Dear Libby,

I'm blessed with many talents. However, all my life I've wished to have a sense of humor. I try so hard but it never seems to work. I crack jokes, sing funny songs and tell silly stores but everyone just looks at me as if I fell from Mars. It really bothers me, especially when I see others say something and they have everybody rolling. How do they do it? Please help, the situation is getting pretty desperate.

Trying Hard to Be Funny

Dear Trying Hard to Be Funny,

You're so intent on being funny, it seems that you're forgetting to have fun. And hey, if you can't have fun telling stories, singing funny songs, cracking jokes, or twisting balloon animals, why bother?

Expressing yourself through your talent, whether it is writing, painting, or humor, has significance in its own right. It is not just for the sake of others, and how they react. It's one thing to want to belong and be the life of the party, but if you want to develop your sense of humor, do so in spite of what others say. Don't develop what's popular to be admired by others, rather, express who you are.

Other people's compliments feel good, it's true. But those bursts of admiration and approving looks are fleeting moments of pleasure.

If you enjoy humor, then go have fun. Let it be stupendously stupid, or hilariously funny. Stand on your head, do cartwheels and somersaults. If humor is something you've wished for all your life, it means that there's something about it that you enjoy. You'll find that if you don't use humor as a way of getting other people to notice you, but rather as something you're developing and expressing, it will be a lot more rewarding. It's better to make a ton of silly mistakes than to allow yourself to be trapped by your fear of whether or not you will gain approval. You do not need anybody's permission to crack jokes or sing songs.

If you can be yourself and express who you are through humor regardless of how it's received by others, you will gain two things. It will liberate your humor from the stress that's imprisoning it right now, and you will find that others will enjoy it more.

Explore humor for the sake of humor, not for the sake of being accepted, admired or popular. Either people laugh or they don't. Live your life and do your thing. Make mistakes. Get it wrong. It doesn't matter. What matters is that you express what comes from you and not how it adds to your status.

Everyone can be funny. There are books, tapes and videos with an abundance of information about any skill you want to try.

Find a funny buddy and swap amusing stories. Listen to comedians. Look at their gestures, their body language, the way they giggle at their own jokes. Practice finding humor in annoying situations by looking at them in exaggerated ways. Yes, some people have more natural humor in them than others, but most of us have more humor than we know.

What we don't always have is the courage to risk failure. Long before we open our mouths to say a word, we tell ourselves that nobody will like what we say.

Maybe they won't.

Who cares?

Set out to explore your own style, express what comes from you. Laugh and add joy to your life. If you find that humor is not your thing, don't be afraid to let it go. Search with an open heart for something that will. Join a dance club, write a novel, paint a picture. A jar that's full has no space, and if expressing humor doesn't bring you pleasure, make space for that which will.

Sincerely,

Libby

Express whatever fascinates you and brings you joy; you do not need other people's blessings to do your thing.

Stop the Blushing

Dear Libby,

I have a problem that I so much want to get rid of. I turn red for every stupid thing, like talking to my teachers and friends. Sometimes they ask me why I am blushing and I start blushing even more!! This keeps me back from talking even though I have so much to say! I'm not even a shy girl. We're making a school skit and I'm a dance-head so you can imagine how I look! It's sooo embarrassing. (It's good that you can't see my face when I write this.) Please help me quick because I can't continue in life like this!

Needs Advice

Dear Needs Advice,

Some people find it harder than others to hide their emotions, so some people cry quickly and some blush involuntarily. If the world would be very kind, then being seen as vulnerable or insecure wouldn't be an uncomfortable issue. When that's not the case around us, we try hard to hide our feelings, to protect our privacy and make sure that no one gets a glimpse of what we're experiencing inside. But when suddenly, our skin gives us away and we blush, or, for some people, tears spill over and makes us feel transparent, we feel as though our privacy has been canceled. Now people can realize that we have emotions. Goodness gracious! It feels like a calamity. That may be why you're expressing yourself so emphatically when you say you can't continue living like that.

Maybe, just maybe, your blushing is in fact, not a misfortune, but a blessing in disguise.

If you're alive, you experience emotions. Like me, like your friends, like anyone alive and healthy. By not being able to hide them, you were granted a wonderful gift, since you were given a greater chance to sooner or later find a way to come to terms with your own emotions. So, if you're scared to say something to your teachers or friends, or to garble your lines in the skit because you might get it wrong, eventually you will find out how to manage this fear. You will acquire valuable life skills along the way and learn how to feel the fear and do it anyway. And in the meantime, you may learn to be okay with the fact that you're scared and can't hide it.

In that sense, the fact that you blush, is an opportunity. It can help guide you toward accepting and cooperating more vibrantly with your emotions. This may take courage, but your courage will help you interact with your emotions, not hide from them; to observe them with respect and curiosity, not with drama or dread.

People are far more moved by authenticity than by facades and smokescreens. Attempts at covering up your feelings can come across as awkward and fake, but realness, a vulnerable sincerity, has quiet resonance that never fails to stir anyone.

Just say what you want to say and say it with all your heart. Share whatever you are compelled to share. If, unlike those who can hide their emotions for much longer, you blush in the process, remember that this will make you into a more authentic person, sooner. Your transparency will become a strength, not a weakness.

Because when we're so keen on hiding our emotions from others, we end up hiding them from ourselves, too. Blushing offers you an invaluable insurance policy to protect you from that. It can encourage you to acquire skills to deal with your emotions, to manage them and turn them into allies, not enemies. You can ask yourself, "Why am I scared of speaking in the first place?" Self-reflecting questions lead to understanding certain things about ourselves. You may learn, for example, that your mind places extreme value on what other people think about you. This insight may guide you toward valuing what *you* think about you.

Once you make peace with how you feel, you'll wonder what happened to the blushing. When we don't feel the need to hide our emotions, do we blush at all?

Sincerely,

Libby

 When we're not so good at hiding our emotions we become good at managing them.

The Heart That Sings

Dear Libby,

My friends know me as the girl who loves to sing, except now I've become too shy to sing around my friends. I have a nice voice,

I just can't bring myself to actually sing in front of my friends. When I do, I choke up and stop singing. How can I get myself to be comfortable enough to really sing in front of friends?

Singer

Dear Singer,

For a talent to develop freely, it's important to put the expression of your singing before the acceptance of others. As a singer, you're a messenger who can bring something to the world through singing. Our gifts, like oranges, come wrapped in a thick peel. It's called resistance, and we all experience it. Resistance is the protective layer that will reason with you, distract you, and prevent you from expressing yourself.

Resistance is experienced as fear and self-doubt. But it also tells you what's inside you. It's an indicator. Your fear points to what you need to do. The more afraid you are, the more you know where your potential lies. That's why we feel so much fear. If it meant nothing to you, you wouldn't feel the resistance. Penetrate the peel, and you'll discover the fruit—sweet, juicy, and rich. Peel back the layers, allow yourself to come out of the cramped insulated corner of personal safety to the possible and the unexpected.

Sing your song, because it's what you truly enjoy doing and allow the rewards to come or not come, for people to cheer or not cheer. Sing for fun, not for fame.

Get to know your voice. Experiment with it. How does it feel when singing alone? How does it feel when holding breath? When releasing breath? When muscles relax and soften? The question becomes not, "What are they thinking?" but, "How does this feel?"

This kinesthetic ability to sense your body will open the possibility for you to truly experience the moment—what athletes call "being in the zone," or performers refer to as, "a state of flow." Sensing yourself—your muscles, your face, your feet touching the ground—will support you even while you risk the impossible-to-predict outcome that triggers fear and resistance.

If breath feels burdened and interrupts your flow of song, gently draw your attention to the air going in and out of your nose, to the rise and fall of your chest, and invite your body to slow down, to become still, to enter a more peaceful state—to feel alive and in the experience. Your voice can then emerge effortlessly. In a calm, living state, your mind and body are full of zip, precisely attuned, everything else fades away as you simply share in song who you are in this moment.

Sincerely,

Libby

 You're most likely to perform at your personal best when the reason you sing is not for others, but for yourself, because you truly enjoy it.

~~~~~~

What Am I Good At?

Dear Libby,

Everybody's good at something and I'm not. I feel I'm worth less than two pennies. Please help me.

Feeling Worthless

Dear Feeling Worthless,

It is our privilege as humans to express ourselves and create beautiful things. Everybody's good at something, and so are you—though you might not have found what it is, yet. To be good at something means you are good at choosing activities that you find intriguing and worthwhile. When you enjoy what you do, you naturally practice it and get better at it. With time, you feel comfortable enough to share with others that which brings you joy.

The question isn't if you're worth a lot or a little, but is there anything you're interested in? Do you feel curious about something, even a tiny flicker of interest? Is there anything you feel drawn to explore? Your interest may be so subtle and delicate, it barely has a pulse. It can be as grand as ventriloquism or as simple as doodling. Pay attention. Allow your curiosity to breathe, to be there. Let it wander if it wants to. Let it move you. Your curiosity is your guide. Follow it. Trust it. Talent is an extension of curiosity.

Expressing yourself is a natural impulse. It's also a personal experience that has a different meaning and significance for each of us. You feel curious about composing songs? Get started. Do you want to decorate pottery? Play the guitar? Dance? Do it. Let curiosity lead you.

Some activities or hobbies we look at and then drop, some we seem to pursue for longer, and others we turn into something that becomes a lifelong passion.

We express our aliveness because this bring us joy. We pursue the activities we enjoy because it makes us feel alive. Do you see the circle? In essence, talent is not something we show, talent is something we express and enjoy. Being good at something means that we enjoy expressing that, and when we do, other people enjoy it as well.

Our gifts, when shared for the goodness of all, become elevated. That's what makes self-expression so rich, so charming, and so magical.

You can't find your talents by staring at what everybody else is doing. You find them by looking deeply and bravely inward, by taking inventory of that which is humming and buzzing inside you—your inherent creativity is right there. You just have to decide what you're going to create. And then you take a step. One small step.

One step leads to many. Soon enough you will find yourself spending some time each day doing what you love. You begin to share that pleasure with others. Not because you care what anybody says, but because what you're doing feels so joyful.

And that joy is contagious. Others catch on. They come and join you. They sit beside you and listen as you sing your song or dance your dance. If you enjoy it enough, believe me, others will enjoy it, too.

Those activities we find engaging and enjoyable are the activities we have the stamina and endurance to practice over and over again until we get good at doing them.

Sincerely,

Libby

 Self-expression, talent, and creativity is what you find when you let curiosity guide you.

Take Time to Explore

Here's a fun activity you can play with to explore your self-expression. See if you can sit comfortably with the questions below, in a state of stillness and relaxation, that is, without a sense of urgency to answer them. Simply create space for anything that comes up for you. As you do that, notice how your mind speaks to you. Does it talk to you through words or symbols? Does it offer colors, images, sounds, music? How do your reflections want to express itself? Is it through song, dance, watercolors, writing? Explore your very own signature style.

- Who is my hero and why?
- What's the most important lesson that my parents, mentors or teachers taught me?
- Which of my experiences did I learn from the most?
- When looking back over the last year, what am I most proud of?
- If I could go back three years and give myself one tip to make life more fun, what would it be?

Once you start asking questions, more may pop up. So take your time. There's no expectations. You are not looking for the candy house of gingerbread, cakes, bonbons, and sugary window panes. You are simply following the trail of bread crumbs, revealing as many as you can find.

Talents in the Corner of My Heart

Dear Libby,

I have many excellent talents, but no one gives me a chance to show them. If I draw a picture, someone else's is bound to be better, and mine goes straight into the garbage can. When my school makes a play, I never get into drama, which I'm great at. When there's a production in which kids my age can act, they won't take me, because I haven't been acting ever since I'm five like others. Is it fair that all my talents should have to sit in a box in the corner of my heart? Please help me find a way to do what I love.

A Cast Out

Dear Cast In,

Some people are given opportunities on a silver platter. They get selected to act and sing and shine. For others, the opportunities are not immediately obvious, but they're there, nevertheless. Because when nobody picks and chooses your talent, you get to pick and choose the ones that will bring you the most joy. It might take more time, you may need to dig deeper, roll up our sleeves, and do some work, but the reward is that much greater.

While the spotlights are on your friends for now, you might discover that to be away from the shimmer of fame for a while will help you find the luminosity inside of you. This may not be your season to reap, but you can decide to use this time to sow, strengthen, and enhance your natural gifts. What are you already good at that you can develop even more?

The acorn holds the seed within that has the potential to grow into a full oak tree. Soon enough, the hard shell cracks open and the acorn begins its life journey. As it grows, it expresses itself at every phase of its life. Every tree expresses its beauty and its potential in its own way at its own pace. When the seed of the Chinese bamboo tree is planted, there's no sign of growth for a very long time. The farmer carefully waters and nourishes the tree, day after day, year after year, with nothing to show for his efforts. Not even a hint. On the surface, there's nothing visible at all. Not a sprout, no blade of grass, not the tiniest bud. Then, along comes the fifth year. Suddenly, the bamboo tree shoots up and grows eighty feet tall in the span of six weeks.

Unseen, buried deep under the ground, the tree's capacities lay dormant for four years. Quietly, without fanfare, it grew underground, developing a root system strong enough to support its potential for robust growth in the fifth year and beyond that will sustain its life as it expands to incredible heights.

While your work may not yet be visible to others, keep drawing your pictures if that is what gives you joy. Through your self-expression, you can communicate who you are to the world and transport somebody else into an experience that only you can create. The famous painter Van Gogh hardly received any acclaim for his work. He continued working throughout his life, not for the success, but for the joy of expressing himself through art. His paintings are now displayed in museums around the world.

If you can support other people in their moments of fame, acknowledging the truth that there's plenty of room for everyone, you will ensure that other people's successes don't weigh you down. Ultimately, you need to stay as light and unburdened as possible in order to sense which type of art wants to be expressed through you.

Sincerely,

Libby

 Talents are about people expressing what they are really interested in expressing.

~~~~~~

Power Struggle and Competition

Dear Libby,

There's a girl in my class who has a power struggle with me or is in a competition with me, whatever you want to call it. Whenever she does something well, for example, when she answers well in class, she looks in my direction to see if I noticed. If we get into discussions, she tries to outsmart me and say something different than I said just to prove that she knows more than I do. We end up arguing all the time. I know that this girl doesn't have the best self-esteem, but still it's driving me crazy. What should I do about it?

Stumped, age 16

Dear Stumped,

Sometimes we are called upon to be strong and courageous, to stay true to our own voice even if another person feels threatened by that. When you express yourself authentically, you share your sparkle. People who haven't yet discovered their own light may feel overshadowed by that. But just because your light feels blinding to others, that doesn't mean that you should stop shining.

Remember that you're like a sun that spreads its light and its warmth for everyone to enjoy. If someone finds what you say valuable, that's great. If they don't, that's too bad. But don't sweat it—you don't have to prove to anyone that your sunshine is luminous or welcoming; don't get sucked into other people's anxieties. If you remove your energy from the power struggle, soon enough the struggle dwindles down and disappears.

If it drives you crazy, that's a sign that you're focusing more on the girl than you are on your own voice. You are no longer expressing yourself but responding to someone else's reactions. Don't allow yourself to get sidetracked and pulled into someone's personal drama. Stay connected with who you are.

If you can understand that behind every attack there's fear, you can feel compassion, and it won't drive you crazy. Think about it. Someone who feels peaceful doesn't try to outsmart or prove you wrong—only a person who is scared defends with aggression. Avoid the struggle. Don't attend every fight you're invited to. Resist the impulse to defend yourself or invest your energies in a fight.

Stay on track with your personal values of kindness, empathy, and your own creative expression. In time, she may discover her own light and realize there's enough space for everyone to shine and blend and merge for even greater splendor and beauty.

Sincerely,

Libby

 If you're invited to a power struggle, you can choose not to join. ♡

When You Feel Shy

Dear Libby,

Please help me. I have a problem that I'm shy by nature, and when I go to a friend's house and her mother asks me questions, I just answer "yes" or "no." I can't bring myself to hold a normal conversation. Whenever I see people, and especially when they talk to me, I'm very nervous. I'm constantly getting butterflies in my stomach, because I don't know what to say. I see my classmates and my family talking to people normally, and I wish I could also. I'm too scared to approach someone about it but I really need help fast.

Afraid of People

Dear Afraid of People,

When people are afraid to talk to others, they're afraid that people won't love them. Usually when people feel shy, they're worried that they won't live up to people's expectations, that their mistakes won't be accepted, and that they will be rejected and unloved. Shyness is about not wanting to put it to the test. That's the meaning of shyness. When I'm shy, it's because I don't want to see what happens in case it goes wrong. I can't handle the fact that maybe people will possibly say, "You? What you just said, oh my gosh, you're so stupid." Shyness is a movement away from the pain of feeling unloved and unlovable.

When you feel shy, what you wish for is a very, very kind person that will love you regardless of what you're going to say or do. Someone like that may be hard to find, but try—maybe a teacher, a mentor, or an aunt can help you feel accepted and loved no matter what you say. In case you can't find one, refer to Chapter 2, and see how you can give yourself a bit more care to find a way out of your shyness. Then you can really start living. When you're living and expressing yourself you wonder less about what other people will do or say, or if they'll accept you, and more about where and how you can grow.

Encourage yourself to add a few more words to a conversation. Chances are that you'll offer something that others will enjoy. You can dare to be pleased sometimes with what you said. And if whatever you said falls flat and nobody responds, or their response is not as supportive, you can always think of it as a worthwhile experiment. Then, you can ask yourself if you've turned into a pile of sand. And if you haven't turned into a pile of sand, you can discover that you've lived through the consequence of people not liking what you said. When you've done that ten times it might not even feel so bad anymore. And, maybe after twenty times, you might think to yourself, "Why am I so busy worrying what other people think? Maybe I should just do whatever I feel like doing, and if they're happy, they're happy and if they're not happy, I know how to handle it. I've done it so many times and haven't turn into a pile of sand, so I think it'll be okay."

Now the only question that remains is what you would like to say. Join in the conversation not so that everybody will nod their heads agreeably, or cheer, but so that you will actually enjoy and have fun sharing.

Sincerely,

Libby

Don't let other people's reactions to what you say stop you from expressing yourself.

~~~~~~

More Talented Than Others

Dear Libby,

Thankfully, I'm smart, and I have a lot of talents: I can dance and sing, I can act, and I can draw. But I have a problem that bothers me. Sometimes I worry that if I'll use my talents successfully, other girls around me will feel inferior about themselves and their abilities. What can I do? I don't want to hurt anyone, but I want to use my talents. I just made friends with a girl who is very cute and nice but I know that I'm smarter and more talented. I want to be nice to her, but every time we get back a test and I did much better than her (she usually doesn't do well) I feel so mean that I'm so smart, and she isn't. Please help me.

Feels Mean

Dear Feels Mean,

You innately know that it doesn't matter how smart or talented you are, everybody deserves to be loved. That is why you feel bad. This is a good and correct feeling. Sometimes our bad feelings guide us in the right direction. You can listen to that, because it tells you that love is unconditional, regardless of somebody's level of smartness or talent. Love is an attitude. You love, when you love life, and when you love life, you love everything that's alive.

Everything that is alive expresses itself and sparkles in its unique way. So, when you're smart, be as smart as you are and give of your smartness to others. When you're talented, continue using your talents and bring them into the service of others. You have it, give it.

Without a doubt, your friend has other gifts, and those are the ones she can give. Because in the end, it's just smartness. And it's just talents. Talents are amazing, it is something we all adore, and we enjoy spending time encouraging each other to develop and express. A life of expressing and sharing talent is a remarkable life to live. But at the end of the day, it's just talents.

Life is not a contest. Every person starts from a different point and is bound for a different destination. Other girls may feel chilled to find themselves in the company of someone like you who is so talented. But often the tortoises who move diligently toward the goal of mastering any ability or skill are those who end up with the winning cup.

So why compare? Just love.

Sincerely,

Libby

 Use and enjoy your talents to inspire others and allow for the talents of others to inspire you as well.

Scared of Copycats

Dear Libby,

I'm always scared of being copied. When I make things out of clay or even just plain drawing art, people always like to copy me.

Afraid of Being Copied

Dear Afraid of Being Copied,

Often, the reason we don't want to be copied is because we think that if we lose our uniqueness we will be less lovable. But true love is given freely. It is not something you can make happen. There's nothing you can do about receiving it or not. The fear of other people duplicating our creations is natural and normal. We want to stand out of the crowd somehow and be special. But maybe we should aspire to know that love is unconditional.

When we know that attention is not love, and that true love is offered freely, independent of what you create or don't, well, why don't you let other people copy you? We're all creative beings, after all, living and expressing our creative instincts. If there's something nice that you do and they copy, that's great. Let them copy it. Enjoy the satisfaction that comes from knowing that your expressions were poignant enough to inspire someone else. Your creations will always be your own and will carry your unique imprint that will make it authentically yours, forever. When we create and share from the heart, it gives others the feeling that you've created it just for them. And when people copy your creations, you know you've hit the mark. Something you originated struck a chord in someone else.

Sincerely,

Libby

 Create original art for its own reward, not as a way to stand out of the crowd and be loved; real love is given freely regardless of what you create.

Final Thoughts

Creative Self-Expression:

The best thing you have going for you is your irreplaceable, available-at-all-times instrument.

And that is: YOU.

Who you are, your own voice and style, is as personal as your thumbprint.

When you express yourself from your heart, you allow others to feel themselves. As they get to know you, they get to know themselves.

All of us want to be inspired by your expression, to be touched in some way. We want to be mesmerized by your music, your dance, your art, or your story.

When You Get Stuck

Creativity cannot be forced, it can only come when it comes. The first stage of creation involves chaos. Before you paint your masterpiece, you sit before a blank canvas. Before we know what to say, we don't. When we run from the chaos, we run from the chance to create. Instead, embrace this tension. It will stretch you. Like a taut rubber band, creative chaos is full of potential. Once released, it will take you far.

Detach your inner creator from your inner judge. This is the type of partnership where each one works best on its own. This is important when you have a developed taste and you know just what you like. Your inner critic can get very active, especially when first attempts don't look like what you had in mind.

Physical activity can help you relieve nervous tension. Take a walk around the block, run, bicycle, do push-ups, or jump on a trampoline to get your body and mind in flow. Once your creative part had its space to breath, explore and express, you can invite your logical mind on board for tasks like organization and accuracy.

Trust Your Artistic Expressions

When you draw or paint a picture from a place deep within you, your art will reveal something that will impact us in a real way. Authenticity is the magnet that attracts those who resonate with your genuine expression. The truth of who you are is hypnotic.

When you sing from your soul, your voice is not like any other we've ever heard. When you tell a story from your heart, your body and your voice become the stage, actors, costumes, music, and props. Watch us, and you'll see how relaxed we become. We get comfortable, lean back and let our jaws drop.

Whatever your expression, know that we're rooting for you, we want you to give it all you've got. What you do and say, will always amaze us with its wonderfulness, or its quirkiness, or its drama, or its humor, or its pain. There's nothing more interesting than the truth. Who could invent all the astonishing facets of who you really are? Trust your ideas, your creativity, your story: your art.

~~~~~~~~~~~~~~~~~~~~~~~~~

Make It Yours

Read the following three quotes. Pick one that speaks to your heart, and get creative. Using colored markers, clay, scrapbooking material, or a musical instrument, see if you can bring your experience to life through your self-expression.

> There are two great days in a person's life—the day we are born and the day we discover why.
>
> —WILLIAM BARCLAY

> Sometimes the smallest step in the right direction ends up being the biggest step of your life. Tiptoe if you must, but take a step.
>
> —NAEEM CALLAWAY

> The marvelous richness of human experience would lose something of rewarding joy if there were not limitation to overcome. The hilltop hour would not be half so wonderful if there were no dark valleys to traverse.
>
> —HELEN KELLER

CONNECT

Chapter 6:

Connect with Others

Life is an echo. What you send out, comes
back. What you sow, you reap. What you
give, you get. What you see in others exists
in you. Remember, life is an echo. It always
gets back to you. So give goodness.

—ZIG ZIGLAR

*A*nyone who is capable of connecting with themselves is capable of connecting with others. Simply by connecting with who you are and expressing that, you enrich and inform and touch the lives of others and draw them to you. The art you create, the music you play, the song that you sing invites others to come and join you. It strikes a chord, echoes back, and harmony is created—a vibrant symphony of personalities and voices, a melodious blend, each one complementing the other. For who can sing in harmony alone?

Connecting with others in mutual expression creates a valuable space where friendship can happen. Each separate thread, rich and vibrant and whole, lovely by itself and beautiful when combined, interweaving to create something new. A new painting, a new song. One song or many, each one enriched by the variety of the other.

This interplay of one voice reverberating on its own and then another, and then together, in a delicate balance of sameness and differences is what makes it so enchanting. When one voice is out of sync or dominates to the exclusion of the other, we produce noise, not music, disconnection, not connection.

Connection is based on the experience that we are all in this life together, regardless of talents, popularity status, or level of intelligence.

We are all one. As you nurture the life in others, you nurture the life in you; when you bring joy to others, you can't help but bring joy to yourself.

A hello to someone at the party, eye contact at the lunch table, a smile, a kind word, listening with genuine care all create music that lingers in the hearts of others and ripples on, impacting people and enriching yourself in so many ways.

In time you'll assemble an orchestra of diverse connections with a variety of friends from different backgrounds, talents, and capabilities that can span many different worlds and bring them together as one. Increasing your circle of friends expands your perspective in life. As you come to see life from different viewpoints, you broaden your own experience.

Because enjoying a range of connections means that you have friends and best friends; when you have best friends, you also have ordinary friends. Both types of connections are significant. Each inspire and elevate us in their own ways.

Casual or short-term acquaintances are fun and exhilarating. Through these connections we can learn to like and appreciate everyone. Long-lasting, dedicated friendships, are meaningful and profound. From these relationships, we learn about ourselves and how much joy we are capable of sharing with someone special: a best friend whose journey runs alongside yours throughout life.

Best friends happen when two people choose to get to know one another in a deeper way because each one senses themselves as more vital, more alive when they're together. When you see the world through your eyes, in your own unusual way, and your friend appreciates your perspective and also adds her own, the space between you becomes animated. It's the discovery of a shared sensibility, coinciding with an added window to another world, that gives a friendship its special spark.

Friendship is a connection between equals, but even as equals we are not always equal, considering that we are human, and we each have our strengths and weaknesses. A mutual friendship, where one friend balances the other is one of life's greatest gifts. Your friend brings out the best in you, and in turn, you bring out the best in her, so what two of you can express together is greater than the sum of the parts.

Such rich and satisfying friendships evolve over time and in stages. They have their ups and downs. We sometimes hurt or disappoint each other, we get things wrong, we make mistakes, and when we find a way to connect again, we build trust through the very act of reconnecting.

When a connection lasts for a long time and is able to withstand its challenges and crises with authenticity, loyalty, and trust, you get to enjoy its finest flavors. You will have created an enduring and truly meaningful friendship.

~~~~~~~~~~~~~~~~~~~~~~~~~~~~~~~~~~~~~

Keeps Switching Friends

Dear Libby,

I have a very good life, thankfully. I have a great family and I do well in school. But there's one thing I've been realizing lately and that is that I keep switching friends often. Is this normal? And how do I develop a good strong friendship that can last?

Needs a Good Friend, age 15

Dear Needs a Good Friend,

There is an honesty about your question that is refreshing: it is a self-reflecting question. You are asking yourself if something is normal and the truth is—how normal is normal? Because we do live in a society where change seems to be the norm. There's always the new kid on the block, the new fashion pair of shoes, the new song, and the new craze that everybody needs to have. Yet, you recognize that something is not quite right about it.

But, if you're prepared to learn how to develop a good strong friendship that can last, chances are that you will find somebody who is equally seeking that. You may need to look for people who can handle your degree of emotional maturity, and that can be a challenge. Every challenge met with courage is a blessing in disguise. It requires meeting with yourself first, becoming your own friend in a way that will invite others to meet you at that level of authenticity.

Good strong friendships that last take time to develop. It's a journey that cycles through different stages.

In the first stage, all we're doing is socializing. Some similarity brings us together, like the same age, the same class, or the same interests. At this level of friendship, all we want is to be accepted and belong. We want to be seen as part of the scene, getting people to like you means everything, and to be cool and popular is the name of the game. This is the *socializing* stage, not yet friendship.

As we spend more time together, we tend to enter the second stage, where we *narrow our focus* toward a particular person with whom we feel some similarity as well as some differences. The similarity brings us together, and the differences intrigue us. That combination is what makes us feel interest in each other, and we start testing whether this could be a friendship.

Gradually, little by little, we move past walls and barriers into a deepening of interest. We allow ourselves to be known more, to be seen in our weakness as well as in our strength. We become a *creative pair*, joining in mutual expression in conversation or through activities. This feeling of closeness is the emerging seed of friendship.

And then comes the *crisis*. This is the fourth stage. For friendship to thrive long term, two people need more than closeness, they require distance, too. At this critical junction in a friendship, the potential for conflict exists for the same reason that the potential for friendship brought them together: friends have similarities and differences. A friendship needs to allow the space for both, to allow each individual to have and develop their own ideas and experiences. This is the stage when fighting and criticism can occur. It's the crisis when the friendship will gain more spark, more electricity and excitement, or prove incapable of keeping this delicate balance.

When this crisis is resolved, and two friends allow each other to be wrong or right, weak or strong, and each one can express the full range of everything they are, they enter the fifth stage, that of *trust*. Without the fear of being judge, criticized or rejected, they are each free to find out who they are, get to know themselves through the other, and grow into their full potential. In this safe space where each can be true to herself and to each other, the friendship just goes from wave to wave to wave and grows deeper and deeper. There can be challenges, there can be mini crises, but, usually, once trust is achieved, they remain connected even when they mutually agree to part ways.

Recognizing this reality—that friendships happen in stages—will illuminate your understanding of how to develop a good, strong friendship that can last.

Sincerely,

Libby

 Friendships go through stages. A crisis, once resolved, holds the promise of a deeper connection.

~~~~~~

Feeling Betrayed

Dear Libby,

Another girl and I are in the same group of six friends, four of whom I'm very close to. This girl and I have had quite a few arguments and fights, but I still thought we were quite friendly, especially since she often comes over (we live close), usually uninvited. But recently, I've heard from a number of friends and classmates that she can't stand me, that I drive her mad, and that she's badmouthing me to all of them. I feel betrayed.

I've already spoken to my mother and have tried acting the same, and probably even extra nice, to this "friend," but it hasn't worked. I can't just pretend that I don't know about it or that I don't feel any resentment, because I do. And I can't just confront her and tell her I know what she's been saying, because she's extremely sensitive and defensive, so she'll probably get very upset and deny saying anything. Please help me fast, because this getting out of hand, and I can't bear it.

Betrayed, age 14

Dear Betrayed,

Betrayal is an act of deliberate disloyalty. But if there was no loyalty in the first place, it's not really betrayal, because there was never a relationship.

This is not about friends, but about people you end up with in the same class. It's about things happening around us. Not everybody is nice to you. Nastiness exists in the world because people are upset, because they're scared, because of all kinds of reasons.

You will experience unkindness in life: rumors, faultfinding, pigeonholing—whatever, because that's what people do sometimes. Don't sweat it. Let people have their opinions. You are definitely not in charge of anyone else's actions.

Because, in the end, it really doesn't matter that much.

Because, in the end, it's just talk.

Not friendship.

There are people that we meet throughout lives with all kinds of interesting agendas. You meet them on the bus, at a dance class, or in a classroom. These are acquaintances, classmates, peers, people. And we needn't call these interactions friendships, and we needn't call them dramatic words like *betrayal*, because they're simply acts that lack kindness because of some people's fears and worries. It's not nice. So? What are you going to do with your life? Respond to everybody that has an upset feeling? Honestly, it's all a bunch of steam. There's nothing going on here.

Go be whomever you want to be, do whatever you want to do. Pursue whatever enthralls you and makes you come alive. Don't stop giving expression to your life, because somebody else has a view or takes objection to how you live. We don't grow beautiful gardens by protecting ourselves from other people's thorns, we do it by nurturing our own roses.

Why fritter away your energy for rumors that pass like fleeting shadows. Today's rumors become yesterday's news. Boring, mind-numbing, and very uninspiring—so why bother?

Use your energy to be productive. Be kind. Connect with yourself, connect with your self-expressions, and connect with others. Spend a full and satisfying month growing and see whether any rumors are of any significance to you after that. See if they still have any significance to take you off the path of growth.

Because when we stop growing, we're bored and everything seems to hurt, and any wind that blows in your direction carries you along with it.

There's a price you pay for that. When you're busy making less of something, less rumors, less upset, less unkindness, you rob yourself from the precious opportunities to make more of something wonderful—more of yourself, more kindness, more friends, more joy.

Sincerely,

Libby

 Invest your energy into building more, not less— more kindness, more growth, and more connections. ♡

Dropped and Replaced

Dear Libby,

I have a friend who used to be my best friend. One day, another girl replaced me in this friendship. Now that she's dropped me, she leaves me out of everything. I really loved her, but I don't know why she doesn't love me.

*Help me. What should I do? I feel so sad. I
don't have a friend.*

Friend Loser

Dear Friend Loser,

Sadness is the hallmark of losing something or someone you cared
about. To lose a friend we once thought the world of can hurt. It
can make you doubt yourself, to feel like there's something not
quite right about you, and to believe that a part of you will never
stop missing her. And yet, every stab of pain that penetrate us,
open us up, invites us to become more of who we can be. In losing
a friend we gain a deeper appreciation of friendship. Consider
whether you've looked for friendship or for simply being liked or
for popularity. How do we distinguish between these?

When we look for a friend as a way to end the pain of loneliness, and to make us feel whole, we soon discover that's not going
to happen. At least not all the time, or in all the ways that we crave.
People, no matter how amazing and magical, are mortal. They
struggle with their own worries and wishes, they agonize, just like
you, about who loves them and who doesn't and whether their hair
is the right style or their shoes are cool, and if they're part of the
"in-crowd."

If you were dropped and replaced, then the question may be
whether you had a friendship to start with. There is a difference
between socializing and friendship. We can have a lot of fun at
parties, and we can laugh a lot with groups, even if nobody is a
friend. You can have thousands of people swaying and clapping
hands at a concert, enjoying the music together, but they're not
friends. They're socializing.

When somebody drops you in that way, that doesn't mean that you've lost a friend, it just means that in the social arena, things are constantly changing and shifting. The flavor of this month may not be the flavor next month. So, don't consider yourself dropped as meaning the friendship has ended, because it had never started. There was a beginning of an acquaintance, a connection, maybe even a kindred spirit, but not yet friendship. If there would've been a friendship, there wouldn't have been a betrayal.

That may be a bit of a bitter pill to swallow, but an important one to recognize. The term dropped doesn't exist in friendships. Friendships can end, because two people can mutually agree that it would be in their best interest. But if another person came along and was found to be, for the moment, more entertaining, or popular, or cool, you may have been the new buddy, the fad of the season, the flavor of the month, but not a lasting friend. Friends don't get dropped or replaced, trends and fads do.

On the other hand, being dropped could be a sign that something is about to happen, an opportunity, a crisis, whereby something cannot stay the way it was and has to break down in one way to be rebuilt in another way. This requires patience to wait and see what happens. A crisis, successfully resolved, carries the potential to reconnect two people on a deeper level.

If you can take the time to pause, to be with yourself, comfort your sadness, explore what your interests are and how you can creatively express yourself, you will be preparing yourself for better friendships—whether this one or another one. If this girl seeks to join you again, then the two of you may be ready for a friendship of a deeper nature. This is a great time to talk about how much you love her and how sad you were when you felt unloved by her. A heart-to-heart conversation at this point, can strengthen your bond a great deal.

Then again, not everybody may be ready for this level of depth in a friendship and you might want to try and pursue connection and trust with someone else. We can't force a friendship, it can only happen when the time and circumstances are right.

Sincerely,

Libby

 When you feel that you were dropped by someone you thought was your friend, consider if this was a friendship or a social fad of the month. ♡

Looking for Popularity

Dear Libby,

I'm not popular but I want to be. Could you please give me advice how I could be popular, and I have a lot of pimples, and I don't like it.

Wants Popularity

Dear Wants Popularity,

Don't chase after popularity. Pursue friendship. Most of us thrive when we have a few good and solid friends, whether or not we carve out a space for ourselves within the "in-crowd" who label themselves as popular.

Making friends is about finding people who enjoy similar ideas, expressions, and activities to yours. It is about connecting. Popularity is not really a feature of connecting; it is irrelevant to connecting because popularity is not friendship. It is a way to finding belonging and acceptance and to feel safe by not being excluded from a group.

Connecting with others means singing together when you and others enjoy singing together, or painting, or playing sports with each other—whatever you love doing. That's called friendship.

Popularity doesn't matter when you have a group of friends with whom you spend time engaging in activities that you love doing together. What's the point of being popular when you have four good friends to fly kites or play guitar with? Who cares about popularity when you're having a great time with a few friends who truly enjoy just being together?

More importantly, explore creative endeavors you would like to express and have fun doing. Painting, drawing, playing football, acting, or twisting balloon animals—discover what you enjoy doing and who would you like to do that with. The ways you choose to express yourself will naturally lead to meeting others who want to express themselves in that way as well. It is one of the most beautiful ways to connect with others and make friends.

Amongst friends, popularity is not important.

Sincerely,

Libby

 Don't chase after popularity. Pursue friendship.

Enjoying a Variety of Friends

Dear Libby,

I have a best friend but the problem is that sometimes I want to play with other people, and then she gets very upset. I don't want to hurt her feelings by telling her this. I don't know what to do.

Doesn't Know What to Do

Dear Doesn't Know What to Do,

It's natural to enjoy spending time with a variety of people. The more you grow and expand your horizons, the more you bring to any friendship. Your best friend can only stand to gain from that.

If your best friend finds this upsetting, talk about it. Don't avoid it. I know, we'd much rather avoid tough emotional or intense situations. We have a tendency to push them away and pretend they don't exist. How's that working for you so far? Seems you've noticed that these strategies don't make the discomfort go away. You're not alone. This is how it is. We can only shove our conflicts and stresses under the carpet for a while; then they resurface when we least expect them to, and often with even more intensity.

Imagine putting this discomfort inside a beach ball. You then attempt to keep this ball underwater, hidden from view, as you smile outwardly and act as though nothing's going on. You may manage for a while, but you can only push the beach ball under the water for so long before it comes surging up and bops you in the face.

We see this often. We don't want to hurt someone's feelings, so we push down whatever makes us uncomfortable; we make believe it's gone. We feel strong, things are under our control, and then, suddenly, boom, anger swells up and a hurtful comment slips out of our mouth.

Instead, when we can find the courage to talk about our conflicts openly, we can avoid inadvertently hurting others. You don't need to blurt it all out. Taking the time to think about it, as you've done by writing this letter, allows you to speak with kindness and respect. You can share with her how much you enjoy spending time with her and how you appreciate having her as your best friend. The more specific you can be about what you like about her, the more she will trust in your sincerity.

With trust established, you can let her know that you also sometimes want to play with other girls and that it has nothing to do with how much you like her; that it's part of who you are to enjoy spending time with a variety of people. Express how you feel about the idea that every person needs the space to be who they are, and that she can trust that when you spend time alone or with others, your friendship hasn't changed, and that you trust her to do enjoy other friends as well.

The truth is that nobody owns you. You are your own person and you get to choose with whom you want to spend your time. When two people can enjoy a nice balance between closeness and individuality without fear of losing the relationship, they have a cherished and rewarding friendship.

Sincerely,

Libby

 It may be tough to share our feelings with the friends you care about and who care about you, but sharing builds trust and helps you grow closer than before.

She Doesn't Have Talents

Dear Libby,

I have a best friend and I really love her. But one problem I have with her is that she doesn't have any talents, and every day she keeps asking me what her talents are, and this causes a lot of fights with her, because I don't want to embarrass her, but I also don't want to lie. And she thinks I don't like her and she keeps saying, "You don't like me, right?"

Doesn't Know What to Do

Dear Doesn't Know What to Do,

Another person's insecurity makes us feel uncomfortable. It reminds us of our own vulnerability. When people feel safe with who they are as a person, and in a friendship, they don't have to keep asking what their talents are or if you like them. The question that begs to be asked is: What does it mean to be a best friend and love someone?

Because you walk together in the school hallway, does that mean you're best friends? Because you have conversations with each other, does that mean that you really love her?

Loving someone means knowing someone. Think about it, I don't know your friend. But there is one thing I know. She has talents. Every single person is blessed with talents. Many! Your friend keeps asking you about her talents because she knows that she has talents. As a best friend, she trusts that you can support her and help her see what's good about her.

Some people are born with special abilities or strengths that become apparent at an early age. Others have been blessed with rare and unusual gifts like limbo skating, extraordinary calculation skills, or having perfect pitch. There are also talents we develop from a natural inclination or a gift we were born with which we study, practice, improve, and express.

You have your talents, skills, and strengths—and your friend has hers. In fact, those talents that come naturally to us are often taken for granted. That's why a good friend can help highlight those talents we don't know are talents.

Talents and abilities come in different shapes and forms. Not all talents are performed on a stage; some are simple, quiet parts of personality. Some people are great at making decisions. Some have an amazing ability to deal with failure. Some people have a knack at seeing the silver lining behind every cloud—they always find the good in any situation. There are people who are great at photography, drawing, creativity, music, juggling and dancing, while others are gifted with the ability to relax, make friends, tell stories, be honest, or manage their time well. Other wonderful gifts include the ability to focus, to make friends, to express yourself, to listen well, to be flexible, to be encouraging, to be attuned to the needs of others. Enthusiasm, empathy, compassion, reliability, flexibility, problem-solving, self-awareness, self-discipline, these are very special talents.

Both you and your friend have unique treasures. Some you were born with, others you honed and developed. If you will look for them, you will surely find them.

Sincerely,

Libby

"A friend is someone who knows the song in your heart and can sing it back to you when you have forgotten the words." —Unknown

I Want to Be a Regular Girl

Dear Libby,

I have always been popular and have always tried to make girls feel a part of it and make them feel that they make a difference, but is seems like girls think I'm trying to be a class queen when I'm really not. I'm a very good dancer, and I draw very well. I'm also smart and have a lot of creative ideas. I'm the most popular kid in my class and almost everyone loves me, but some kids think I'm a snob. I just want to be a regular girl in my class. Please help me.

Not a Class Queen, age 15

Dear Class Queen,

When others make us into an icon, like a class queen, it means that people have seen in you certain qualities that other people would like to be part of. Many people like to follow someone who seems to know what she's doing. Often it gives them a sense of comfort and security to feel led by someone who is strong and kind. Still, if others have placed the mantle of leadership on you, you can choose whether or not you want to assume that role.

The simple answer, of course, is just to say no, I just want to be a regular girl. Then you're off the hook. You can step down from this position and into the background until your title disappears. All you need to do is get on with your own business and do what you do quietly for six months, and you won't be queen anymore. It's not difficult to accomplish that.

This is not always a dishonorable choice. Many people take that route out of angst, insecurity, or simply because they just can't be bothered. That's totally acceptable. Sometimes it's easier to be a hidden leader in the shadows and enjoy a different calling.

If you do want to express yourself and share your gifts with the world, your natural leadership abilities and charisma will prevail. And then you may need to assume that role humbly and joyfully.

To do so, you need to understand what that role means. Because a queen doesn't take on the heavy yoke of living other people's lives. She simply shares her gifts. She doesn't take distance, or rank herself above others, but connects with her people. She's patient, she acts in the face of fear, endures adversity, and accepts that not everyone will adore her. She doesn't show off but dedicates herself to mastering her skills.

She influences others by her own example.

She is recognized by other queens—those who are kind and strong and confident in themselves, who have also assumed this role humbly and joyfully. As a team, they bring out the best in each other and what they create in the shared space together, is greater than the sum of the parts. In this way, they enhance their own lives and enrich the lives of others.

Sincerely,

Libby

A queen displays courage and doesn't do things for status or approval alone. She knows that to be kind and understanding is more rewarding than to be important. ♡

How to Make and Keep Friends

Dear Libby,

I have trouble keeping friends. I can't understand how or why it happens. One day I'll make a new friend who seems to like me. Then just when I start to think, "Wow, I actually have a friend!!" she picks another girl or all of a sudden, she thinks I'm weird or neglects me. I don't know if I should feel happy that I lost a bad friend or feel sad that I lost a good friend. I really don't know what to do anymore. I try to be thoughtful, friendly, cheerful, and fun—without overdoing it, though. I can't take this pressure and sadness. (Sigh.) Please help me, quickly!

Can't Keep a Friend

Dear Can't Keep a Friend,

There are certain areas in life where you really can't succeed unless you're *not* trying. Try hard to be calm and relaxed, for example. Would that work? The harder you try, the more stressed you become. Sometimes, the harder we try to pursue friends, the more we are, in fact, pushing them away.

You've tried keeping friends for a long time. It didn't seem to work. Maybe it's time to try letting go and see how that works.

Maybe it's time to stand back a bit, to stop running from the fear of being alone. Fear urges us to run, but you can see that as we run away, we run into new problems. It's like, we run from loneliness, then run into problems with friends, then run from that in an ongoing cycle.

Stopping this kind of running, or from trying too hard, doesn't mean that you're giving in or giving up. It just means that you take a pause to discover what you want. "But how?" You may ask. "What should I do in the meantime?" These are fair questions we all ask ourselves.

Sometimes the answer is that you need to become your own good friend, first. If you do that, you will have a friend for life who will always be there for you and never leave you. If you can accept yourself, rather than wait for others to do that for you, it will be a lot easier for others to follow suit.

Find out what you're good at and what you enjoy. Find out if you treat yourself like you would treat a good friend. Do you appreciate your unique self? Or do you neglect yourself? Is there a voice in your head that tells you that you're not good enough, or weird? Ask yourself if this is something one friend would say to another and discover how you can be more supportive and caring to your vulnerable, inner self.

Have fun with yourself. Explore the world through your eyes. What are your interests? What are you curious about? What are your values? When you're comfortable spending time alone instead of seeking to not be alone, you can connect better with others.

Making friends, like falling asleep, is best pursued indirectly. Just as spontaneity or happiness or catching a bubble in your hand happen best without pressure or force, so too, satisfying and enduring friendships happen in a relaxed, easy-going manner. When two individuals share the activities they enjoy, friendship happens. When you sit and play with tunes and melodies for a while together, you create harmony.

Friendships is what happens between people, through mutual conversation or activity.

Join the space where activities happen. When people are drawing join them in drawing, when they're playing ball, join the game, when they're having a discussion, join the conversation, when they're not doing anything, see if you can suggest something you can do.

When you're having fun together, connections happen. You find people who enjoy what you enjoy. Often these connections tend to end when the fun is over and the novelty is no longer there. Sometimes, however, when you meet somebody you get along with, you spend lots of time sharing activities together, and you then get to also share values and beliefs. You get to know this person, you develop trust, you open yourself up , and you discover that you're friends.

Deep bonds happen this way. And they last.

Sincerely,

Libby

Friendship is what happens in the space between two people—in the movement, in the action, in the process of self-expression.

She Gets on My Nerves

Dear Libby,

I used to be good friends with someone in my class, but now she gets on my nerves. She always has something to object about whenever I say something. Sometimes we bicker about the silliest things like where a store is—if it is on an avenue or street. I want to cut my relationship with her. Should I do it, and if yes, how?

Used-to-Be-Friends

Dear Used-to-Be-Friends,

What are the options when two people fight? Either you make up with each other or you end the friendship. Both of these options have one requirement, and that is that you need to love them. You need to connect. Sometimes you connect on a deeper level and sometimes you connect in order to disconnect.

New friends are always exciting and interesting. There's a sense of mystery about someone we don't know yet. We wonder about their lives and what remarkable things have happened to them. We hope that we'll be able to learn from each other and grow in new ways, and we dream about the interesting things we can have fun doing together.

As time goes by, and we get to know them a little more, some of that mystique is lost. If, in the beginning, it felt like our friend can do no wrong, we suddenly find out that they're human after all. They make mistakes. They may hurt you, they may disagree with you or ignore you or do something that can make you wish that you will never see them again.

We live in a time where we don't have to fix our stuff, just buy new stuff. So we don't learn how to care for something over time. When friends don't fulfill our expectations, we give up and go looking for a new one.

Tossing a friendship is the easy way out, but this often creates a cycle you're likely to repeat: meet new friend, spend some time together, something goes wrong, leave, and repeat the steps. You pay a price for that, too. Once your heart is hurt, you close yourself more, protect yourself more, erect walls and barriers to shield yourself from pain. It becomes very challenging to feel really close to another human being.

To be clear, if someone is physically hurting you, damaging you, or in any way being violent, then, absolutely, you need to say no. You need to tell an adult, get help, stop the aggression. But when this is not the case, and your running, climbing trees, escaping the imaginary threat, you're in a state of survival, not living.

Our built-in security system doesn't know anything else but to do that: escape immediately. And its solutions are always fast, half-baked solutions, quick fixes, unrealistic tactics that never really work. We come up with smart ideas, sometimes, but hardly wise. Instinctive, impulsive action can be common sense, even logical, but often, it's based in fantasy, wishful thinking and lacks sophistication. It doesn't see the big picture, and while it may fix one difficulty, it brings more problems in its wake. This is how it goes:

> Run from your friend.
> No, I can be all alone! Grab a new friend.
> No, she's not kind, run. No, no, no, no!

Most of us are running around saying no all the time, because we don't even know what we do want. We become, "I don't want," people, creating one strategy on top of another, on top of the other, and we've long forgotten why or how it all started and what's really bothering us.

To know what we do want, to find our yes, we need to pause, to be still before we make our next move. There's very little ability to know what we want if we're not paying attention to what's going on in the moment. Only when we can face what we don't want, can we know what we do want.

And when the mist clears, and we stop running, often what we can see then is that the threat we thought we were running from feels every bit as threatened herself. All she ever really wanted was a little bit of assurance that she's okay, that she's liked, and maybe she demanded too strongly or too loudly or too awkwardly.

So, before you break out in a run, take a break. Before you disconnect, connect.

No one guarantees that she will participate—not everyone is capable of connecting, but you can do this one-sidedly as well. It's not the common thing to do—not among teenagers, not even among adults, but it is the right thing to do. And for the rest of your life, you will know how to maintain relationships, and how to end them, when necessary, with peace in your heart.

Sincerely,

Libby

 Before you disconnect, connect.

Arguing about Everything

Dear Libby,

I used to be good friends with someone in my class, but lately we started arguing over every little thing. Sometimes we have entire debates about the stupidest things. I want to stop being her friend, but I like her. Should I drop her or not?

Friends-That-Were

Dear Friends-That-Were,

It's nice when our friendships coast along. We understand each other, agree with each other, do things together, and have fun. In reality, every friendship, like everything in life, has periods of ups and downs and everything in between, even in the best of friendships.

It isn't fun or easy—knowing that when things are up they may soon be down, for example. But there's comfort in knowing that things in life like seasons and friends can have cycles of closeness and distance. Because if you can't learn to travel comfortably alongside the waves of fights and friendship or rest and playtime, then you'll have a hard time building long-lasting connections.

And that would be a pity, because friendships get better with age; they ripen, open up and become more splendid and miraculous. It's what we all want.

In the harmony around us, there's a natural pattern of beauty that flourishes and shrivels, swells and shrinks, moves forward and back, circling and spiraling and constantly in motion, just as the waves ripple on and the wind sways to and fro. Things change and situations shift and people grow, and we can learn from our experiences. We simply don't gain anything when we stay small and get stuck in petty arguments.

Sometimes, precisely because we like each other, tempers flare. It's because we care. When you don't especially care about someone, you can stay indifferent a lot more easily. If a friendship gets a bit tempestu-ous, and you weather the storm, it has the potential to bring you closer than ever before.

In all situations, whether it's the ups or the downs, there's some-thing to be learned, something to be gained. It's the stupid—not just the smart, the failures—not just the successes, the fight—not just the fun that teach valuable lessons.

So, yes, hang in there.

Sincerely,

Libby

 The ups and the downs, the fun and the fights, the failures and successes, each phase offers its own value.

To Be Spiritual or Friendly

Dear Libby,

Sometimes I feel a burning desire from deep inside my soul, to grow and become a very spiritual person. But I have a big problem because something inside me tells me to do bad things and not to become very spiritually great. Also, my friends are very immature, and they don't think so deeply into why we are living—why we were created and

put on this world, so they often make fun of
me and my serious view of this word.

Sincerely, Wants Spirituality

Dear Wants Spirituality,

When we face an intersection, we automatically assume that we need to choose one path. How can we be on two paths at the same time?

Wisdom, however, sees the paths from a higher perspective, a higher vision (think of a helicopter hovering above). The more you can synthesize, or bring together, two seemingly differing tracks, the more you can see that there is not just one path. You can find the relationship each path has with the other. Wisdom looks for connection—for the point where two roads converge.

Spirituality is not about escaping our humanity to become an angel in the sky. Everything physical can become spiritual, our thoughts, our feelings, our speech, our actions our joys and our sorrows are connected on every level, because nothing is without meaning and purpose.

You feel a burning desire to grow and become spiritual, while at the same time, you feel, "something inside me tells me to do bad things and not to become very spiritually great." Spirituality is not about removing yourself from the world, but about living in it, with it, and for it—to become fully human and master your instincts and impulses keeping them in your hip pockets to use wisely.

Humans have the ability to live on two spheres, with the mind above growing in wisdom and deeper aspects of life, and the heart below, pumping life into our physical needs, desires, and sensations to survive in this world. When both these capacities, the human and the spiritual, work in sync, we experience the world as one harmonious whole.

As a matter of fact, how can you be good when you don't know what bad is? And even when you're good without being bad, how are you human at all? As much as you have a burning desire to be spiritual, you also have the hunger to eat a sandwich, you have instincts, impulses, and urges that seek pleasure and avoid pain.

Spirituality connects humanity; everything that brings people together and unifies and strengthens the whole, is spiritual, everything that creates discord and disconnection and dissonance is not. But if your friends represent all the bad and you want to embody all the good, the spiritual, how can you team up?

Any kind of search for spirituality that separates you from others and sets you apart is probably human nature disguised as spirituality. As you see the bad (or human nature) *and* the good (or spiritual) in your friends *and* in yourself you will create a harmonious whole. To be spiritual is to be whole. When we find our own wholeness we spontaneously find the wholeness in others.

All our natural emotions and human impulses are here to guide us and teach us. To grow from instinctive and impulsive actions (what you call bad) to finding a balanced and measured way to deal with our human drives is the spiritual journey humans undertake.

It is only when we have the courage to see things as they are, the physical and the spiritual, that we can reconcile our human nature with holiness and find how each has something to contribute to the other.

Let's consider this a bit. Every single person is unique and special, with a combination of qualities different from every other person alive.

When do our differences disturb us? When we're not secure with our sense of self and not clear about our own path. When we know who we are, differences intrigue us, and we learn from the differences.

When we work on spirituality, we become sensitive to it and find it difficult to tolerate its lack in another person. Say someone is conscious about authenticity. Hearing someone coloring the truth can greatly disturb her, which may lead to conflict.

So, how can we grow in our spirituality without letting our difference divide us?

By understanding that we may develop in a one area while our friend may develop in a different area. And we can look out for that, and respect that person's growth and development.

The pathway to spirituality begins as a personal one. Each individual perfects herself, culminating in the perfection of every part of the whole.

Sincerely,

Libby

As you become one with yourself, your human nature and your divine essence, you will become one with those around you. That is spiritual.

Lonely without a Best Friend

Dear Libby,

I have a class of twenty-five girls but I don't have a best friend. This makes me feel very lonely and sad, because I don't have someone to discuss my problems with. Can you give me advice on how to make a best friend?

Lonely, age 13

Dear Lonely,

Instant friendships, like instant food, do not last for too long, nor are they truly satisfying.

Best friends are about two people who feel close to each other because of mutual interest and trust that has developed over time, not overnight.

To have a friend is to be a friend, and it is in your power to be a friend. Best friends are not about having a friend but demonstrating that you are one. Maybe it's going the extra mile for someone, maybe it's listening with patience and understanding. Be that person to others. It goes both ways. If you're somebody that people would want to talk to, you're more likely to find somebody amongst the twenty-five classmates to talk to. Who could you support and enjoy time with?

It can be as simple as smiling at someone one day, saying "hello" the next day, and writing a kind note the week after. The way you act toward others will be reflected back to you, and others will respond in kind. Giving of yourself to a friend is a true expression of living. In the very act of giving, you experience yourself as passionate, alive, and brimming with joy. When you focus on giving rather than needing, it is likely that friendships will follow.

Sincerely,

Libby

Share your time and attention with others, make their lives happier and more meaningful, and you will be able to call many people your friend. ♡

I Changed Schools

Dear Libby,

I changed schools this year and my new classmates are already friends with one another. Could you please give me advice on how to also make friends?

Thank you,

Needs Friends, age 15

Dear Needs Friends,

Approach one girl at a time rather than focus on the whole class. Start with a girl who you feel shares similar interests to yours, such as a favorite activity or hobby. Discuss these interests with her; ask her some questions about it. Invite her over to your house and spend time doing something pleasurable together.

To have a friend is to be a friend. If you look around, you will notice others who are lonely too. Focus on making others feel good, and you may find that you will acquire your most meaningful friendships.

Sincerely,

Libby

 The whole class is not a person, so it's hard to make friends with it. Instead, start by making connections with one person at a time.

Final Thoughts

What's Your story?

Once upon a time . . .

Remember when you used to snuggle under the covers and wait in delicious anticipation to hear these magic words?

So, what's your story?

Stories are a fun way to connect with anyone. It's also a very respectful way to share something with your friends. Using stories, we can say things we sometimes don't know how to say.

Telling someone, "You should be more patient," is different than saying, "I want to tell you a story that happened to me." Everyone relaxes when you say that, even the most defensive people. When we're calm, we become curious. In this engaging way, we allow our words to paint images on the canvas of the mind. It invites others to decide things for themselves. "Hey, I know what the problem is. My impatience is making things worse."

Storytelling is a very nice way to connect with others. So is story-listening. Because when we tell a story, it often sparks a similar story in someone else's mind and conversation begins to flow.

In telling a personal story, we allow our friends to recognize that in some way you are just like them and have the same feelings and the same struggles. It creates a bond of understanding and trust.

In listening to a story, we validate our friend's pain and discomfort, joy and pleasure. It creates feelings of empathy and kinship.

Stories That Are Ready to Go

Take some time to reflect on a story you can have in your hip pocket. Get a notebook, a recorder, or a friend who will listen, and describe the milestones and experiences that have brought you to this moment. There are many ways of telling stories, but the ones that have a beginning (set up), middle (a conflict), and end (climax and resolution) are usually the most satisfying.

If you'd like to get creative and play with your story, explore these four possible stories:

- **Discovery:** How did you discover the talents you have used and enjoyed until now?
- **Bumpy road:** What were some obstacles you faced, mistakes you made, weaknesses you discovered in you, and how you overcame these challenges and grew into who you are now?
- **Success story:** How did you use your gifts and talents and skills to solve a problem that you were faced with?
- **Your vision and your dream:** What do you see in the world that activates in you a desire to do something that will add joy to others? What message do you want to share with people? What difference do you wish to make? What do you want to create?

Putting It All Together

When you have some ideas, here's a simple way to put your thoughts in order:

1. Describe the situation
2. Elaborate on the action
3. Reveal the result
4. End with a thought that lingers

Here's an example story from my life that uses each of these elements.

1. When I was in elementary school, my father went bankrupt. His business had failed, but not his spirit. The only thing that went

through his mind was what would be his next step. He decided to sell sweaters.

2. During the next few years, my parents hosted many interesting business acquaintances in our home. Over my mother's piping hot, delicious food, my father shared stories with buyers from Saks Fifth Avenue, Bergdorf Goodman, Bloomingdales, Macy's, and Lord & Taylor. He told stories about common struggles we humans face with a sense of suspense, a sense of humor, and an unexpected ending. The stories were always heartwarming. And the buyers always ordered plenty of sweaters.

3. When I graduated from high school, I went to work at his company. I was responsible for preparing the piles of checks for deposit to the bank. My father's sweater business (and his stories) were generating millions of dollars in sales.

4. When I asked him how his stories turned into sales, the question seemed to puzzle him. It wasn't that his stories didn't create sales. It was that he didn't think of his stories as a business strategy. He sees value and pleasure in a casual business meeting, because he simply likes people. He has a knack for sharing the right story with the right people at the right moment. He is a connector.

There isn't anyone you couldn't learn to love once you've heard their story.

—MARJORIE PAY HINCKLEY

GROW

Chapter 7:

Keep Growing

The creation of a thousand forests is in one acorn.

—RALPH WALDO EMERSON

*E*ach of us has an internal impulse to become more of ourselves. Think about the oak tree. It starts out as nothing more than an acorn. A seed. But it has the full potential to become a tall, sturdy oak tree. In the same way, we all have everything we need for the specific purpose we were designed to live up to.

In fertile soil, with enough sunlight and water, the little acorn begins to take root and sprout. It grows. It starts to develop its own identity, and it becomes a sapling, a young tree. The roots then push deeper into firmer soil and grow more solid and sturdy, and the tree reaches out, taller and wider, expanding its branches day after day. Then one day, it becomes the mighty oak tree, standing tall and proud in its full magnificence.

Now the tree has reached the stage where it wants to give back to its environment, to the world that nurtured its growth and development. It provides shade, offers a home for animals and birds, and produces seeds, more acorns, to produce more oak trees.

Just as the acorn contains the mighty oak tree, the seed of your potential lives within you and around you. Growth is a natural instinct. We all want to explore the possibilities of what lies ahead of us, to get a glimpse of what's around the bend and over the hill, and to learn more and more. There is no end to how much you can grow!

When we grow and apply our knowledge and practice our newfound learning, we integrate it and weave it into the fabric of our beings. As with riding a bicycle, repetition leads to mastery, creating a pattern in the mind that allows the new insight or skill to become more automatic and consistent. This in turn frees up space to focus on more learning and further growth.

In time, our mind begins to make connections between diff-erent patterns of learning. It uses information from one understanding and puts it together with something else you've learned, connecting the dots. This synthesis adds to our creativity, and enables us to take leaps, to create new patterns from existing patterns, so that we don't stay stuck in one pattern. That's why creativity initially involves imbalance. When things are in balance there is no creativity, because there's stability and constancy like a wheel that keeps turning in steady motion.

Creativity happens when things get out of balance, and we must to reach a new balance. Until we can find a new balance, we experience disharmony, dissonance, conflict. This creative chaos is an integral part of the growth process. This generates tension because a part of us prefers the familiar, and a part of us wants to evolve and grow into new patterns and further balance. We like stability, but we need growth. Growth, however, cannot happen unless there's discomfort or conflict. If we don't let go of the old there cannot be any new. That stage between letting go of the old and acquiring the new is a state of imbalance.

We grow from stage to stage through a period of crisis. A child that crawls on the floor and wants to start walking on two feet will go through a crisis. This in-between stage, when crawling is no longer desired, but walking is not yet fully developed is the stage of crisis. When the child can walk there is again balance, quite literally. Later, when the child wants to learn to ride a bike, that becomes the new crisis of growth.

Any child who wants to learn to walk or ride a bike, will keep their eyes on the prize, enduring short-term pain for long-term gain. So too, when we grow into what we are capable of being, we need to invest time, effort and energy, but the reward is always increased joy and fulfillment.

The pathway to growth begins as a personal one. Everyone expands into her unique role with her personal mission. Each individual enhances her own qualities, expressing another facet of life and then sharing that with those around her. Recognizing and appreciating the qualities of others and the gifts that they bring, culminates in the harmony of every part of the whole—infinite, evolving, as yet unfinished.

~~~~~~

Wants to Say Sorry

Dear Libby,

Every single time I get frustrated or stressed, I get into a tizzy and start saying mean things and screaming. After this I feel bad, and I want to say sorry, but I don't know how.

Confused

Dear Confused,

Saying sorry is a skill. We're not born knowing how to apologize. It's something we need to learn and practice to become good at. You clearly understand regret: that there is something you have done that was impulsive and shouldn't have been done. Lots of people find themselves doing impulsive things; not so many are aware of their regret, and even fewer know how to say sorry.

The stronger we become in understanding and being ourselves, the easier it is to say sorry. To acquire this skill, see if you can turn it into a research of sorts and ask different people how they do it. When do they do it? Is it hard for them? What helped them? Experiment with the ideas you learn and you will find out for yourself how it feels and what makes it possible.

Let's talk about this for a minute. When we want to say sorry, we want the other person to accept the apology and to be kind to us, and then it will be easy to express regret for something we have done wrong. But often, when we say sorry, it's because we see the pain we've caused, and then we're worried that the person won't like us or will be upset with us. That's a possibility—people may be upset. So, we're afraid to be rejected for what we've done. Ultimately, however, it is we who will feel better if we say sorry when we need to, even if the person doesn't accept the apology. We will feel that we have done our part.

Saying mean things and screaming is easy. So is eating ice cream. Apologizing and getting along takes effort and skill.

Instead of running from the fear and discomfort, simply pause, breathe, see how still you can be as you let those intense feelings move through you. Fear cannot sustain itself forever unless you feed it. So, even if it feels like the storm will never pass, it does. You say sorry, and you realize you haven't been laughed at. Your friend accepts your apology, and you become better friends because you worked through it. You can stay in charge of your fear. When you do this, you can experience the calm and peace that follows.

Skills like these tend to accumulate and draw to them more skills. They attract more growth. Once you get good at saying sorry, you will become skilled at other things, like resisting impulsivity in the first place.

Sincerely,

Libby

 It's not that we're supposed to know how to do things right, but that we learn skills with practice. The more adept you become at a skill, the more you can grow into other skills.

~~~~~~

They'll Find Out

Dear Libby,

I'm in eighth grade and I don't do well in school. My test marks are pretty low no matter how much time I study. My mother wants me to learn with a tutor. She's very nice and is helping me a lot, but I'm embarrassed to tell my friends. Whenever they ask me where I'm going, I make up a different excuse. I'm so scared that soon they'll find out the real truth, and then they won't want to be friends with me anymore.

Scared

Dear Scared,

When we discover the limits of our capabilities, what can we do? All of us have our own personal limitations. You are asking how to deal with the fact that if you learn at a different pace than everybody else, how will you be accepted by others and not be considered as stupid? The real question is not how we avoid our limitations, or hide or run from them, but how do we address them?

It may be that you believe that if your friends find out about your tutor, they would not want to hang out with you anymore. I'm not sure they would care, though. But even if they do, you are doing the right thing by learning with a tutor. Many people absorb information better when they study one-on-one with a personal teacher.

The first step is to be okay with the truth. Then you won't have to run from it.

When we're young, our parents, and our family, envelop us in a warm and cozy cocoon of security, like fledgling chicks in a comfortable and familiar nest. Then, as we grow older and step out into the big world, we naturally look for a warm and cozy center, a place where we can belong in society. Sometimes, society comes toward us, weaving that sense of security around us, and sometimes it doesn't, leaving us with the task of creating it ourselves.

When society does it for us, and we get that security on a golden platter, that's wonderful, but at the same time, we possibly miss out on an opportunity to discover who we are as an individual. Being part of a group gives us a sense of identity. If I belong to a drama club, for example, I might not feel the need to belong to myself.

Sometimes individuals are excluded from a group because of stigma or bullying, or because they're developing their skills at a different pace than others. But while they lose the security of the group, they gain a greater chance to find the security within themselves, to draw from somewhere inside them a sense of safety. This happens because they are more motivated to learn about who they are and who they can become.

However, this blessing in disguise can be squandered when we become overly preoccupied with our social status. By chasing after belonging and acceptance, we may end up losing just what we've been pursuing. It's like trying to grasp a wet bar of soap: hold it too tightly and it slips out of your hand; hold it too loosely and it falls. A desperation to find security in belonging and stressing out about your friends discovering your secret tutor is a way of trying to control people's attitudes toward you and may actually harm your friendships.

If you can ease up a bit and let go of your friends' opinion of you to find security in yourself, then, ironically, your chance for acceptance and belonging will be much greater. How can you find security in yourself? By shifting your focus from *them* to *you*. Take all that energy you've been directing toward hiding and making up excuses about where you're going and channel that to your own growth and development. Take pleasure in your progress, in the fact that you're growing. Enjoy it.

As long as you're scared of losing your friends and concerned with what others think about you, it is hard to address what you need to grow. If, for the sake of belonging, you let go of you own self-development, then you'll probably lose both, you'll chase after others which will remain elusive and your own development will suffer. Hold on to your self-growth and you will have both—belonging and self-development.

Sincerely,

Libby

 Don't try to control the people around you, see how you can nurture your own growth.

Let's Unwrap the Gift

Trials and tribulations are gifts in disguise. They help us discover hidden strengths. Few people achieve anything great without first overcoming a few obstacles.

Challenge yourself to find one gift in a situation you've been resisting. If you allow yourself to face the issue and grow from it, the wisdom hidden within it can open the door to a new world. What has been hard for you in your life? What troubles have you needed to address? Every experience is a gift.

Find a photo of yourself that reflects your sweetness, innocence, and beauty and place the photo where you can see it while you're thinking about this. Then, let your mind recognize and accept a difficulty you're having and ask yourself:

1. How is this difficulty a blessing in disguise?
2. What can I gain from facing this challenge?
3. What choices can I make to deal with this?
4. What have I learned so far about this, and how do I feel about it now?
5. How can I turn this "stumbling-stone" in my path into a "stepping-stone" for learning and growth?
6. Who or what can help me grow from this challenge?

Know that all of the answers you will ever need reside within you. These questions are merely an opportunity for you to access your own wisdom.

> "When you are inspired by some great purpose . . . your mind transcends limitations, and your consciousness expands in all directions . . . Dormant forces, faculties, and talents become alive, and you discover yourself to be a greater person by far than you ever dreamed yourself to be."
>
> –Patañjali

Growing Together, Not Apart

Dear Libby,

I have a major problem. I have a friend who is overly studious. She studies for quizzes and tests for hours and starts weeks in advance even though she knows the material without studying. This is causing her lots of stress and really ruining her life. I feel it is my responsibility to let her know and help her with this major problem. She is also putting lots of pressure on everyone around her. I feel extremely pressured from this and study for more than I need to and have time for. Due to this fact, my confidence is being destroyed. Please don't tell me to stop being friends with her, because she's an amazing friend with a great personality and a true friend. Please help me quickly . . . school is beginning soon.

Cares-About-School-but-Not-So-Studious

Dear Cares-About-School-but-Not-So-Studious,

In friendships, it is usually our similarities that draw us together, but our differences are just as special. A good friend doesn't mean an identical twin. What we want is a nice balance of sameness and differences and that's what makes the space between us so fascinating.

While you admire your friend and appreciate her personality, it is totally unnecessary to stop being friends just because she studies differently from you. It is the creative and animated combination of the familiar and the strange that buoys a friendship and helps you grow and develop. Your differences can be very complementary and help bring out the best in each of you, so that what you two create together is greater than the sum of the parts. Together you can discover your strengths and develop yourselves in a way that neither one could accomplish alone.

Friends can influence and shape each other's outlook. But the way to go about it is to show, not tell. People generally don't like to be told what to do. More importantly, it is not our place to take responsibility for other people's attitudes or actions. We can, however, take responsibility for our own attitudes and actions and how we affect others. Your approach toward learning and studying makes sense. You care about school and see it as an opportunity to grow and learn. Your friend seems to be studying, not just to learn, but in order to succeed or impress others.

Anything that will highlight the differences between two friends can create tension. If managed well, this kind of tension can actually energize a friendship and unite you in new and interesting ways. A car moves forward by the wheels which apply resistance against the road. When you move in the opposite direction to the way your friend is moving it can motivate and inspire her to learn from your style. Shift your focus from the way your friend studies to pursue your own path. It's easy to be pulled along by her style and make her pressure your own. Instead, you can lead the way and be an example. Gently resist her intensity and stay cool and confident, secure in the knowledge that your manner of learning is the way to go.

Sincerely,

Libby

The same energies that can drive two friends apart are the same energies that can bring them together and encourage them forward.

She Thinks She's the Best

Dear Libby,

I have a friend who thinks she's the best. She has to impress everyone and is very bossy. When I talk to some other girls, she looks at us like: you guys are so dumb and don't know what the right thing to do is unlike perfect me. When someone asks her a question, she looks as if it's a bother to her royal majesty and answers it as if: get away from special me. The most annoying thing is, she thinks she can do all this and still be my friend. It is hard for my real friends and for myself. What shall we do?

Stuck in the Middle

Dear Stuck in the Middle,

When we have two opposing fears that pull us in conflicting directions, we feel stuck. You don't want to be with this girl, and you don't want to be without her. You're angry at some things she does, but you're afraid of letting go. You may have a wish to fix her or make her change or act differently, but you're not sharing your thoughts with her, and you don't want to confront her either. You see, if you don't like spending time with this girl, all you need to do is walk away. But you're not walking away, you keep looking at her. So, you're stuck in the middle between these opposing forces.

How do we get unstuck?

One way to free yourself is to redirect your focus from things you don't want and find out what you do want. Once you know what you want, you have direction. Who are the people you do want to connect with? What kind of values do they have and how do they act? By following what you want, you'll be actively pursuing goals rather than running from that which you don't want.

Another way to get unstuck is to identify the trigger that's keeping you rooted to the spot and not allowing you to be who you are. We often tend to feel upset about somebody who wants to make themselves more visible than everybody else. Why does it bother us? When we have a perception that the light that shines on people is limited, we're afraid that we may lose some of its glow. So, we compete for this "scarce" amount of light, all based on an inaccurate belief. Whether or not we participate in this competition is our choice.

In truth, of course, there's no limit to the light that shines. Humans can be each so unique that we can all be seen and distinguished by the special light that we bring to the world, without having to fight over it. Nobody can do YOU, quite the way you do YOU. In fact, the more we develop ourselves, the more we radiate our uniqueness to the world. Interestingly, when we enjoy our process of growth and development, it no longer matters whether somebody sees you, because you're visible to yourself. You know who you are and you know who you want to become.

Sincerely,

Libby

 Grow and develop your most powerful device: You. The light you are meant to shine into the world is yours alone, as individual as your fingerprint, as personal as your voiceprint.

~~~~~~

A Number or an Actual Person?

Dear Libby,

I have a massive problem that's really weighing me down. I go to a high school where there are many students. Like in most big schools, I find myself becoming more of a number than an actual person. No one notices me because I'm good, and I get no attention whatsoever!

Lost in the Crowd

Dear Lost in the Crowd,

It's great that you're not chasing after negative attention. While it's not easy to be left without any attention, getting the wrong kind of attention is clearly a very bad solution in the long term.

The question we need to ask ourselves is: Do we want to be someone in the eyes of others, or do we want to be—in your words—"an actual person" in our own eyes? When we're very young, we all want to be someone in the eyes of others. It's what makes us feel accepted and loved and safe. There comes a time where we recognize that usually people are occupied with their own self-protection, looking for love and safety, too. Unless we outgrow this instinctive way of being in this world, it's hard for us to see another person for who they are.

What do we do when we're in a school or in a family or in a city, where we don't get noticed by others and we feel lost in the crowd?

229

We need to discover for ourselves that we're not a number. When we find ourselves, we no longer feel lost. To explore that a bit more, you can refer to chapter 1 in this book.

Finding ourselves leads to growth. As we develop we move from self-protection and survival to living and thriving. Growth naturally leads to increased visibility—a rose is more visible than the seed beneath the ground. But the secret to real joy lies in growing for your own sake, not for the sake of the crowd. Growing for others, to be somebody, or to be under the spotlight for a moment, becomes very draining and is very difficult to sustain.

If you want to be free to grow and express yourself in your unique way, strive for authenticity rather than safety. Because when we grow for the sake of others or to belong, we all tend to grow in the same way, into the same person. Like clones, we dress the same, speak the same slang and try to squeeze ourselves in to the size and shape of others. And in the end, you find you were not true to yourself. There's another approach. Instead of following the crowd, grow in a way that suits you—that fits your interest, your mind and body and capabilities—regardless of whether or not others will see and accept you.

If you do get noticed, well, that's an added bonus. And often it comes. People are very intrigued by individuals who grow in their own flair. It has a felicity of style and grace which makes it both noticeable and inspiring to others. Some people may come and join you for a while, participate in your song, your art, your dance or your music, and then they move on, and others come to take their place. And that's wonderful, because you are always there with you, enjoying your own self-expression and growth. And that's what truly matters.

Sincerely,

Libby

Don't wait for the crowd to find you, find yourself—the individual—and grow into your full potential.

Bad Crowd

Dear Libby,

Two years ago, I became friends with a crowd that does bad stuff. My mother warned me not to be friends with them, but it took me so long to make friends, and I didn't want to be without friends. Recently, though, something happened and the girls all suspected that my mother had told the school about it. My mother said she didn't. I believe her. I told the girls that, but now they ignore me and say really horrible things about me and also about my mother. I've told them to stop, that it's hurting my feelings, but they just laugh. How can I leave them and make new friends again?

Friendless

Dear Friendless,

Do you remember the story of the trapeze bar in Chapter 3? When you don't let go of the bar behind you than you cannot move on to the next bar. How do you let go of friends is not difficult to answer. You just let go. How do you trust that you will have new friends—that's the difficulty. Facing the chasm between the part of you that wants to be safe and the life inside you that wants to grow takes courage. The fear of possibly not making new friends is fighting for your survival. But, of course, survival and living are not the same thing.

If this crowd is not right for you, it's not right for you. We all need to recognize when we have outgrown something and need to develop into something greater.

When we grow, we wonder whether the future will bring whatever we want it to bring. But unless we let go of the past, we can't discover what the future has in store for us. Some people look forward to trying new things. Others, so many others, avoid taking a leap of faith. They fear that they'll be judged and rejected, that they'll fall and break. Letting go doesn't mean that you don't have self-doubt. It means that you believe that you can figure things out. It means that you trust more deeply in the skills that you have and your ability to develop any skills that you lack.

Go more deeply and bravely inward. Take an honest inventory of the skills you already have. Noticing that this crowd isn't right for you is in itself a skill. It means that something inside you already knows what the right crowd is. It's not so bad when we discover we've been exposed to something that wasn't quite right, because it can help us understand what is right. Often, it's when we experience the wrong step, that we understand the right one.

Grow into the crowd that you know you should be in. If it isn't there, initiate it. You're the one who can create it, because by under-standing what it shouldn't be like, you know what it should be like.

You can look beyond what comes naturally to you—hanging on to the old bar—and take the leap into growing. Go out there and spread kindness and joy. You can shape the crowd. The truth and the knowledge that you've gained from your experience can add value to the crowd in a wonderful way.

Sincerely,

Libby

 We can only grow to the next level if we're ready to let go of the previous one. 🤍

Feeling Useless without Goals

Dear Libby,

I feel so useless in life. I don't have any goals to accomplish. I don't see any reason why I'm here in this world. I feel like no one cares about me. I'm either being used to help someone or just ignored. I'm not a good student, maybe even dumb. I have no true friends I could tell how I feel. I wish I had a puppy or something like that. At least he might listen and give me comfort. Please help me.

Feeling Useless

Dear Feeling Useless,

You want to be useful and that's good but finding somebody to care about you is not related to your usefulness. You are and always will be important just for being you. You are a gift to the world.

You see, real care is given freely and not because of goals we accomplish. Some people see goals as those set by others for you to achieve in order to receive care. (An excellent report card will reward you with a pizza party, or playing a perfect piece on the piano will shower compliments upon you.) But, when others truly care about you, it has nothing to do with goals. It's important for you to separate care from goals. Care is something you receive regardless of the goals you've been given or have accomplished.

The truth is that you matter just the way you are. While you are loved and supported, and people indeed care about you, sometimes others are preoccupied with the pressures and distresses in life, and you feel alone. You have much to offer. Maybe you can find somebody, an aunt or a kind neighbor, or maybe a puppy—who you can connect with so that you feel more comfort. If you don't, refer to the conversation about caring for yourself in Chapter 2 of this book.

You say you don't have any goals to accomplish. This is because you didn't set any goals. Maybe you thought goals are set by others, which you then do, in order to receive care. Now that you know that goals have nothing to do with care, make a list of goals. Set them. Accomplish them. And then make another list. Before you know it, you will feel useful.

Goals are about identifying what you want to do and finding out how you can bring more joy to yourself and others in a meaningful way. When receiving care is the whole point, we stay small and limited, too busy figuring out how to please those who may offer some approval. But every person can move from goal to goal and feel useful and fulfilled, because the joy of growth is more satisfying than any compliment.

Do you want to become a better student? Do you want to have better friends? You want to get a puppy? Amazing. These are wonderful goals.

What steps can you take to get you there? Write them down in order of priority. Take your first step, just one step and start building momentum. If your next step is too high, you can't climb to reach it; if it's so low that it's a no-brainer, you won't feel like you're stepping anywhere. That feels useless. Maybe the first goal you can accomplish is to ask yourself what is your next step. Any step. It can be a step toward learning half a page of math, or finding a tutor, or a friend, or striking up a conversation with the girl sitting next to you in class.

Useless is not something we are or we aren't. It is an outcome of a wrong definition of goals. Everybody can be useful if they define their single next step.

Sincerely,

Libby

 Separate goals from care. Care is a wonderful feeling that is offered freely. Goals are something we set for ourselves in order to express, grow, and add joy to ourselves and others.

Belief Upgrade Ladder

The choices you make and the things you do create the person that you are becoming from moment to moment. If you believe that the patterns of the past determine your future, then you will cling to them. But the truth is, you can recreate yourself and choose to define yourself in other ways, any time you want. You can upgrade your beliefs in a gentle manner, without fighting them, but by adding words that soften and calm them, like: "Maybe I can." Or, "What if it is possible?"

Here's an illustration of how adding something to a limiting belief can update your mind and increase your freedom of choice.

I don't have what it takes.

Maybe I have more than I can see.

What if I do have all it takes?

I have what it takes.

I have more than what it takes!

~~~~~~

Between Two Friends

Dear Libby,

I have two best friends who don't get along with each other, and by recess and lunch I don't know who to talk with. I don't want to hurt anyone's feelings. I just want everyone to get along.

Stuck In-Between

Dear Stuck In-Between,

We're often faced with conflicting expectations coming from two people we enjoy spending time with. When that happens, our first impulse is usually to try and please both. But it's challenging to always meet everyone's wishes, especially when they are opposed to each other and speaking to one friend will come at a price of upsetting the other friend.

We live in a world where the people around us look toward us to feel special and loved. This places a burden on us, because when we don't supply that need, they tend to get upset. If we take responsibility for other people's experiences, we end up feeling like it's our fault. Any time we do something, even if our actions are positive, meaningful, and growth-oriented, other people can have their own view about them, either positive or negative.

When we intend to go through life and avoid all discomforts, we inadvertently end up feeling a lot of distress. In this case, you are feeling stuck because you're faced with two potential discomforts, and you do not see a way to resolve both. You sense that if you speak to one friend it may disappoint the other and vice versa. So, you're at a loss as to what to do, because you don't want to upset anyone, including yourself. It is natural that you would want to avoid any discomfort and that everybody should just get along, so you can feel calm and peaceful. But that's not always in our hands.

Often when we feel stuck, it's because our mind is busy thinking up different suggestions to avoid any kind of pain, but at the same time, we know that every path away from pain leads to another pain which cannot be escaped. We find ourselves running in circles, because we don't know which path would be best to take. So, what are we to do when discomfort cannot be avoided? The answer might sound surprising.

When you feel uneasy and stuck, redirect you search for a path away from pain, to choosing a path toward growth, pleasure, and joy. This means you may have to accept that there will be some discomfort. Giving up the path of running from discomfort is easier said than done, but it's very rewarding. You can develop your ability to tolerate discomfort, to endure pain, to know that discomfort is inevitable, and that you have the capacity to bear it. So, sometimes you will speak to one friend and bear the discomfort of the other's reaction to that, and sometimes it will work the other way around. It is however your choice to express yourself and grow through conversation in the way you feel drawn. If somebody gets upset about that, you will do your best to endure that, but don't stop your self-expression and your growth.

You might even share your dilemma with your friends and tell them what you plan to do about it. You can let them know that your choice is not based on who's more important or less so, but rather that you follow the direction of growth.

When you choose to move toward growth and not the escape from pain, your friends may be inspired to do the same, and eventually you will, perhaps, all connect as a threesome and grow in that way. That would be great. But choosing the path of growth often takes courage. Sometimes people around you might choose not to be friends with you because you've also chosen another person. If that happens give them time, but if after a while they remain caught up in their path of non-growth, then, regrettably, your growth probably lies elsewhere.

In friendships we can add to other people's good feelings about themselves, but we cannot be responsible for their need to feel special or safe or secure. We can only pursue growth, and find others that do the same, and share the journey.

Sincerely,

Libby

 When you feel uneasy or stuck, redirect your search for a path away from pain. Choose a path toward growth, pleasure, and joy.

Wants a Hobby Fast

Dear Libby,

I am so bored. I want a new hobby and fast! Some of my friends like to paint, draw, sing, and so on. I tried sports, dancing, sewing, knitting, needlepoint, hook rug, outdoors, and more. There's nothing to do. All day I sit around and do nothing!!! It is sooo boring. My mother said hobbies just come up,

*but they don't for me. I just can't stand
being bored all the time! Please help, fast.*

Needs Hobby and Fast

Dear Needs Hobby and Fast,

Your mother is right, hobbies just come up. You can't force a hobby—
that would no longer be a hobby, which is something you do for
pleasure or relaxation. When you feel pressured about doing something, it hardly allows for spontaneity.

Hobbies are the whispers of your heart. It's different than routine,
say, when you tidy up your room or do math equations. To listen
your heart's calling, you need to be still, not in movement.

You seem to be desperately running from boredom. Boredom may
be uncomfortable, but it's not life-threatening, is it? As long as you
see boredom as your enemy from which you must flee (like a war
refugee) how can you have the peace of mind to listen to the still
quite voice inside of you that knows what you would enjoy doing,
what you're meant to be doing?

When we look for a hobby or explore what kind of activities we
would enjoy doing, we will generally experience chaos. So many
options to choose from. So many voices in our head telling us we may
fail, others will laugh at us, and that we're not cut out to do the things
we feel drawn to do. This creates dissonance. And it's uncomfortable.
As you know from Chapter 3, we can't get rid of discomfort quickly,
we can only add comfort.

Your opportunity for growth lies in this stage of creative chaos. It
is your moment. You can absolutely step into the ability to dwell in
this unknowing, to accept boredom, to do nothing.

Until you know what to do.

Only in a state of stillness can we find flow—to feel fully engaged and animated in activity you enjoy to the point where you seem to lose the sense of time and space. It's like that special feeling you have when you're looking at the beauty of a sunset or the breathtaking view from a mountaintop. You feel good. You feel alive. You don't just sing, you become the song, you don't just write a story, you live the story. In flow, you are in the moment, doing what you love to do.

So, while you're impatient to find a hobby fast, maybe you can have fun trying out what non-movement feels like. It sounds so simple, it almost can't be true, but it works. Try it. How long can you sit still and just feel the flow of air moving in and out of your nose? Even five minutes of that is worth its weight in gold. It can seem like nothing, a granule of sand in a vast world. But granules of sand form mountains.

See how long you can caress a plant or observe fish in a tank. How long can you simply look through a window? Go on a *noticing walk*, just stroll through your neighborhood and notice things you haven't seen before. Pay attention to all the sounds you can hear—birds chirping, the swish of a soft breeze or the ripples of a child's laughter.

From this state of rest and relaxation, you have the best chance of listening to your curiosity and to follow that impulse. Don't try to force anything, your hobby will come up in its own time.

Sincerely,

Libby

 Learning how to be still is a skill that anyone can learn. Stop moving. Unless there's an actual danger to your life, gently resist the impulse to act. Instead, allow time to be still.

Not So Smart

Dear Libby,

My whole class is very smart, and I'm not that way, and in order to do well, I need to study with smart people. That's not fair because they get a good mark anyways, and I need to depend on them to do well. My teacher even gives me easier tests. The problem is that she makes it very obvious and everyone knows and talks about it. They make fun of me, and I'm hurt and embarrassed.

Desperate for Help

Desperate for Help,

Anyone who seeks solutions to challenges they're struggling with is smart. It's the smart people who can admit when they don't know something. They're the ones who can muster the courage to say, "I don't know something." or "I need some help." In contrast, there's nothing very smart about making fun of, hurting, or embarrassing another human being.

Doing well on a test tells you how smart someone is at memorizing information, it doesn't tell you how smart someone is at using what they've learned in real-life situations or at understanding the feelings of others.

Everyone is smart in different ways.

The question is not how smart you are, but rather, how are you smart?

Some people are smart with using words, some with numbers, some with images or patterns, and some are smart in the way they can relate to other people with empathy and kindness.

Everyone can take their particular set of smarts and build on them. If you're good with images, see how you can use that ability to help you study for your tests. Maybe you can draw sketches of what you learned or imagine a scene unfolding on the stage of your mind to help you remember. If you're smart when it comes to movement, try walking around or dancing while you study. If it's music that stimulates you, use songs or jingles to help you remember facts and numbers. If you're good with words, see how you can explain what you learned in your own words, either to friends or to your mirror. Have fun learning.

So, if your whole class is smart, you are too. You just need to find how you're smart. Find the talents hidden in you. Maybe you excel at things you've never even thought about. Are you good at cutting hair? Skiing? Running? Baking pie? Are you good at cheerleading? Calming yourself down when angry or afraid? Bicycling, bird watching, Zumba, photography, scuba diving? No kind of talent or smarts is silly or unworthy or too weird.

Find where you're smart, and then what others have to say won't matter that much.

We all have our strengths and our weaknesses so we can learn and grow and share with each other. If someone helps you study for a test, you might be able to offer her some creative ideas for her writing assignments or art project.

You know, as you read these words, that you're really smart—in your very own way. You don't need anyone's permission for that. See your imperfections as learning opportunities and remember your unique capabilities.

Sincerely,

Libby

 Everyone is smart differently. Find how you're smart and build on that. ♡

Seeking Confidence

Dear Libby,

*I am fifteen years old, and I feel that I
have no confidence in school. I'm scared to
say anything in the classroom. I always blush
and think that the class will make fun of me.
I'm very quiet altogether, even at recess
or after school, and especially in public. I
feel like I'm so complex, and it makes me
depressed. Please help me fast because I'm
beginning to hate school.*

Wants to Be Confident

Dear Wants to Be Confident,

Confidence is an outcome of learning and acquiring skills. As you learn, you develop your skills, talents, and potentials. Then you feel confident. Confidence is a result.

But when confidence becomes the goal, it's hard to learn.

We are all complex. We're all gifted and talented people who, in the corners of our hearts know the person we might become, the work we can accomplish, the painting we can paint, the song we can sing, the dance we can dance. And if we would sit still long enough to listen to that voice, we would be captivated by its call.

But we also have fears, self-doubts, and suspicions. We suspect our own shadows. And we run away from our gifts because we're so scared of being judged as different, or amazing, or peculiar. But no matter where we run—there we are. We can't really run away from ourselves.

The class, or the public, or quite simply *they* who you imagine will either embrace or reject you, is really a mosaic of individuals who are just as worried as you are, too busy protecting their own hearts from being hurt to worry about yours.

When we feel afraid, we look for an escape. In the process we run from ourselves, and we run from those running from themselves, and then we run from the running itself. So, maybe what you're looking for, and what you're calling confidence, is a break from the running.

Perhaps it's time you do take a break. Pause. Breathe. Look around the room, and you'll see that there's no one out to get you. Sense your feet on the ground. You are safe.

When you stop running, you can begin learning. You can dedicate yourself to gaining knowledge and increasing skills. You can expand your mind and try new experiences and approach your lessons with a sense of wonder and curiosity.

Resist the question about what everyone is thinking of you, or how they will react, and if they will accept you or not. Start to engage in the learning and focus on growing. This will give you confidence. Explore those subjects that interest you, practice skills, develop your capabilities, and you will feel competent. Confidence will come. It happens spontaneously.

Confidence is a result. It's the shadow of learning; it follows you wherever you grow.

Sincerely,

Libby

 Dedicate yourself to learning, not to impress, and confidence will come. ♡

Final Thoughts

Engage with Your Emotions to Grow

Emotion is an energy that drives movement (as in *e-motion*, energy in motion). When your emotional mind perceives danger, it drives movement away from pain. When it identifies pleasure, it drives movement toward that. You can be the participant in the emotion, or the observer of it. You can let the emotion *use you* to serve your survival operating system that wants to keep you safe, or you can take charge and *use* your emotions to grow.

Instead of moving *away* from pain, see if you can move *toward* growth. Here's how:

- **Movement:** Use a physical movement that your brain associates with the emotion (i.e. breathe while sensing your chest and tummy moving up and down = calmness. Softening your forehead and the muscles in your face, allowing the softness to spread to your hands = resting energy.)

- **Create a soothing environment:** trigger the experiences that your mind associates with emotions that are calming, soothing, and uplifting. (i.e. light a scented candle, play relaxing music, or view a photo of a beautiful scene.)

- **Heart holding:** bring your palm to your chest to remind yourself to breathe, slow down and comfort yourself.

~~~~~~

Make It Yours

Affirmations

Positive thoughts can reprogram our thinking patterns so that, with time and repetition, we begin to feel—and act—differently. The affirming words below are some examples you can try when you want to add calmness or growth and feel more relaxed about friends. You can copy them on a card and tape to your mirror or wall, or place in your purse to carry along. Have fun creating your own, using words that resonate with you to affirm the areas of growth you want to cultivate.

For Calmness:

I sense the breath flowing in and out of my nose.
I breathe easily and deeply.
My breath is gentle, rhythmic, and nourishing.
I am safe; all is well.

For Growth:

I can do it.
I am competent and skillful.
I welcome and learn from my failures.
I see my imperfections as learning opportunities.
I trust the process of my growth.

For Friendship:

I have many wonderful friends.
I love my alone time. I support and uplift myself.
I love and support others.
There's always a friend for me.

WISDOM

Farewell

~~~~~~

Wisdom Is a Process

*I*n the end, questions often lead to more questions. You may have found some answers to your questions about friendship within these conversations—different perspectives, insights, and life skills—that may stimulate questions of your own. That's wonderful. Questions are opportunities that lead to growth and wisdom.

Growth and the pursuit of wisdom may take work, but it makes life joyful and meaningful and adds so much to our friendships. It gives us inner freedom—the ability to choose our responses within the space we share with our friends, and for that matter, in any situation.

Remember that wisdom is a process, not an answer. The wise person knows how much she does not know and constantly seeks to listen and learn from others.

Wisdom is transmitted from generation to generation. Knowledge about what creates harmony and dissonance, what creates comfort and pain, what connects and disconnects, what creates balance and imbalance is passed on through culture. Every generation adds more wisdom.

Sometimes we find answers to our questions and feel a sense of comfort, and we don't want any changes to come along and disrupt the equilibrium of our lives. Change is, of course, inevitable. In fact, the inevitability of change is one of the only unchanging features of life.

Wisdom guides us through these shifting tides toward har-mony and balance. This requires patience and stillness. With time and practice we learn to dwell in the *not* knowing for a while, bearing the discomfort of the question and developing the capacity to hold two or more opposing ideas in our minds. Wisdom will emerge.

As you access wisdom, you will live your life with empathy, compassion, and kindness toward yourself and others. You will become a vessel of joy overflowing with caring and understanding to those around you. Wisdom is a blessing in your life inasmuch as you become a blessing in the lives of others.

That's it for now, my friends. We've come to the end of our journey together. We've explored different viewpoints, some may have helped you understand yourself better, others may have helped you understand people around you better. Some of the questions may have been more interesting than others, or more useful than others, and may apply at certain times more than at other times. I hope that the conversation about questions will help you appreciate the value of asking. As you make your way forward, *your* questions will guide you to *your* inner wisdom and lead you toward enriching and meaningful friendships.

Farewell,

Libby

About the Author

*L*ibby Kiszner is a weekly columnist, author, educator, and a mother of nine. Over the last fifteen years she has answered close to two thousand questions in her column. She has written several books to a wide audience of readers from different cultural backgrounds.

Libby senses and cherishes the vitality and potential in every living creation. Her personal life and work are deeply infused by the belief that reconnecting with our most authentic selves inspires us to become meaningful givers, devoting ourselves to the wellbeing of others.

THE HEART OF THINGS

Libby

About Familius

Visit Our Website: www.familius.com

Join Our Family

There are lots of ways to connect with us! Subscribe to our newsletters at www.familius.com to receive uplifting daily inspiration, essays from our Pater Familius, a free ebook every month, and the first word on special discounts and Familius news.

Get Bulk Discounts

If you feel a few friends and family might benefit from what you've read, let us know and we'll be happy to provide you with quantity discounts. Simply email us at orders@familius.com.

Connect

- Facebook: www.facebook.com/paterfamilius
- Twitter: @familiustalk, @paterfamilius1
- Pinterest: www.pinterest.com/familius
- Instagram: @familiustalk

FAMILIUS

> The most important work you ever do will be within the walls of your own home.